KU-630-594

The Beginner's Guide to
DOG AGILITY

Laurie Leach

The Beginner's Guide to Dog Agility

Project Team
Editor: Stephanie Fornino
Copy Editor: Joann Woy
Cover and Interior Design: Mary Ann Kahn

T.F.H. Publications
President/CEO: Glen S. Axelrod
Executive Vice President: Mark E. Johnson
Publisher: Christopher T. Reggio
Production Manager: Kathy Bontz

T.F.H. Publications, Inc.
One TFH Plaza
Third and Union Avenues
Neptune City, NJ 07753

Copyright © 2006 by T.F.H. Publications, Inc.

All rights reserved. No part of this publication may be reproduced, stored, or transmitted in any form, or by any means electronic, mechanical or otherwise, without written permission from T.F.H. Publications, except where permitted by law. Requests for permission or further information should be directed to the above address.

Printed and Bound in China

06 07 08 09 10 1 3 5 7 9 8 6 4 2

Library of Congress Cataloging-in-Publication Data
Leach, Laurie.
  The beginner's guide to dog agility / Laurie Leach.
     p. cm.
  Includes index.
  ISBN 0-7938-0546-5 (alk. paper)
  1. Dogs--Agility trials. I. Title.
  SF425.4.L43 2006
  636.7'0888--dc22
                              2006000287

This book has been published with the intent to provide accurate and authoritative information in regard to the subject matter within. While every precaution has been taken in preparation of this book, the author and publisher expressly disclaim responsibility for any errors, omissions, or adverse effects arising from the use or application of the information contained herein. The techniques and suggestions are used at the reader's discretion and are not to be considered a substitute for veterinary care. If you suspect a medical problem, consult your veterinarian.

The Leader In Responsible Animal Care For Over 50 Years!™
www.tfhpublications.com

Table of Contents

Introduction 4

Part One: Laying the Foundation

1. Falling in Love With Agility 9
2. How the Game Is Played 19
3. Selecting Your Canine Partner 29
4. Keeping It Positive 41
5. Building an Obedience Foundation 49
6. Pre-Agility Training 61
7. Going to School 71

Part Two: Training for Agility

8. Learning the Obstacles 81
9. Teaching the Jumps 85
10. Teaching the Tunnels 97
11. Teaching the A-Frame and Dogwalk 107
12. Teaching the Teeter 127
13. Teaching the Table 135
14. Teaching the Weave Poles 143
15. Handling Skills 157
16. Sequencing 171
17. Training Challenges 183

Part Three: Competition

18. Getting Ready to Trial 199
19. Packing It Up 207
20. Your First Trial 213
21. Minding Your Agility Manners 227
    Afterword 232
    Appendix I 234
    Appendix II 244
    Resources 249
    Index 250

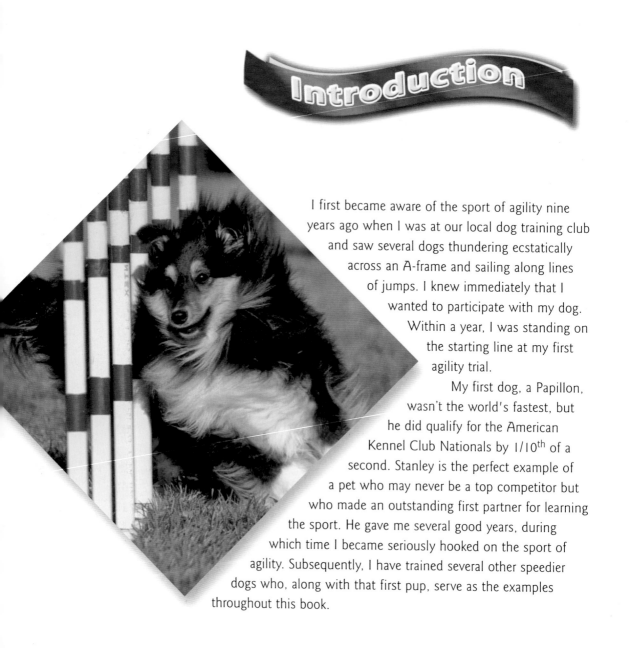

Introduction

I first became aware of the sport of agility nine years ago when I was at our local dog training club and saw several dogs thundering ecstatically across an A-frame and sailing along lines of jumps. I knew immediately that I wanted to participate with my dog. Within a year, I was standing on the starting line at my first agility trial.

My first dog, a Papillon, wasn't the world's fastest, but he did qualify for the American Kennel Club Nationals by 1/10th of a second. Stanley is the perfect example of a pet who may never be a top competitor but who made an outstanding first partner for learning the sport. He gave me several good years, during which time I became seriously hooked on the sport of agility. Subsequently, I have trained several other speedier dogs who, along with that first pup, serve as the examples throughout this book.

Tucker is a large Papillon with good speed. He is extremely ball focused and will work for anyone who carries his favorite ball. Tucker serves as an example of how to train a dog who loves toys.

Scout is a high-drive Shetland Sheepdog. She growls with excitement during her runs and barks in frustration when she has to stop. This gal sees agility as her life's work, and she will do anything in agility if I communicate it clearly.

Grace is an athletic, fast Pembroke Welsh Corgi who loves to run and is getting ready to debut in agility. She will serve as my model for the dog who wants to play but whose body type adds extra challenges.

Agility is immensely important to me. I compete two to four weekends a month, generally with more than one dog. I experience a wide range of powerful emotions from playing this game—joy, despair, and excitement. After racing sled dogs for years and training in competitive obedience, I am convinced that agility is the most fun you can have with your dog. I hope that as you read this book you will have the same thought I did many years ago: "Hey, I want to do that!"

Above right, from top:

Stanley is the perfect example of a dog who made an outstanding first partner for learning agility.

Tucker, a large Papillon, serves as an example of how to train a dog who loves toys.

Scout is a high-drive Shetland Sheepdog who thrives on solid communication with her handler.

Grace is an athletic, fast Pembroke Welsh Corgi who exemplifies the dog who wants to play but whose body type adds extra challenges.

Introduction

Part 1

Laying the Foundation

Chapter One

Falling in Love With Agility

Since its creation in the late 1970s, agility fever has swept through dog lovers across the United States and around the world. Virtually every recognized breed and many mixed breeds are competing in this sport and earning titles, and five major organizations in the United States alone are sponsoring trials. What is this activity that has captured the heart and soul of dog trainers around the world?

Agility is a competitive sport designed to test a person's training and dog-handling skills over a timed obstacle course. Competitors race against the clock to direct their dogs through tunnels, over an A-frame, across a dogwalk, and through a line of weave poles. In short, agility is a very exciting event for participants and spectators alike.

It is important to note at the very beginning that agility has the potential to be much more than just another hobby. When you fall in love with the sport, you join a large community of dog lovers who are passionate about this complex game. In a matter of months, you may find yourself unable to pass an open field without checking it out as a potential agility course. If you live in a hillside home, you may find yourself looking longingly at houses with flat yards. Even if you have never built anything, you may find yourself surrounded by epoxy and pieces of plastic pipe used to construct agility jumps. When you make that first call to find out about an agility class, be aware that you are about to embark on a wonderful adventure with your dog as your partner.

A Revolution in the Dog World

Agility has a fascinating history. The sport began as a filler event. At Crufts Dog Show in England in 1977, organizers were concerned about keeping the crowd interested between classes. Committee Member John Varley, who had a background in horse show jumping, questioned whether an obstacle course similar to those used in that sport could be set up for dogs. Varley invited a working dog trainer, Peter Meanwell, to design the first agility course, and by the 1978 show, the game was ready to go. Two teams of four handlers and their dogs wowed the crowd with their blistering speed as they completed the course. Agility, as it came to be called, was born. Little did Varley or Meanwell suspect that they had created a sport that would revolutionize the international dog world. Today, the history of agility is still revealed in the convoluted courses and the scoring of faults patterned after equestrian show jumping.

Virtually every recognized breed and many mixed breeds compete in agility.

Laying the Foundation

Training to Compete

In writing this book, I am making one significant assumption. That is, if you decide to participate in agility, you will eventually compete. Although you could train indefinitely and never enter a trial, this is exceedingly rare. Once the agility bug bites, most people become eager to try out their skills at a show. This is important to note, because agility competition requires you to select your canine partner carefully, and you will need to train in a way that is more methodical than just playing in the backyard with a few obstacles.

How the Game of Agility Is Played

Agility is a team sport, with the team consisting of a human and canine partner. Together, the team must negotiate an obstacle course at a brisk pace. The challenge of the game is to complete all the obstacles correctly within an established course time. The handler's job is to tell the dog where to go next on the course, and the dog's job is to complete each of the obstacles as fast as he can.

Agility courses are designed by agility judges who rely on guidelines established by the sponsoring organization, such as the American Kennel Club (AKC) or the United States Dog Agility Association (USDAA). Although courses may have similar elements, each course has variations that make it unique.

Skill Levels

Agility teams progress through skill levels from novice to advanced, with each level becoming increasingly challenging. At the novice or starter level, courses include 13 to 15 obstacles and are generally fairly simple to negotiate. These courses are designed to show that the dogs have mastered the obstacles. At the intermediate and advanced levels, courses average 18 to 20 obstacles and require teams to perform complex maneuvers and discriminate among obstacles placed very close together.

Class Organization

Dogs are organized in classes by height, and they are measured at their withers to determine how high they must jump. If you have a very small dog, he might jump 8 inches (20.3 cm). A large breed might jump 20 inches (50.8 cm) or more.

Agility Speak

Agility has a vocabulary all its own. Throughout the book, watch for an explanation of key terms under the Agility Speak heading.

Obstacles

A variety of obstacles are included on each course, including tunnels, an A-frame, weave poles, a dogwalk, and a teeter-totter. During the run, the handler cannot touch the dog. However, she is allowed to give verbal commands, point, and use body language to get the animal to negotiate the obstacles in the correct order and under the maximum course time.

Scoring

Judges score the dogs' performances as they run each competition course. Knocking bars off jumps, completing obstacles in the wrong order, or failing to perform an obstacle safely results in penalties. On each competitive run, a dog either qualifies or disqualifies based on the number of penalties accumulated and the time it took to complete the course. Dogs who qualify earn "legs" toward degrees that are equivalent to a high school diploma, college degree, and doctorate. Dogs who don't qualify can try again at the next competition.

Who Can Play?

One of the attractions of agility is that anyone who can move quickly can play. At a typical trial, you will see junior handlers (those who are under 18) and senior handlers. You will see lightning-quick handlers and slower handlers. You will see able-bodied handlers and handlers with disabilities.

Of course, handlers must do their best to stay close enough to their dogs to show them the correct obstacles. Slower handlers can compensate for their lack of speed by training their dogs to work farther away from them. Even at the national agility competitions, you can find competitors of all ages and fitness levels. The bottom line is that if you want to try agility, get out there and give it a go. Even if you never compete, you and your dog will become closer friends.

There are a variety of obstacles on an agility course, such as the teeter-totter pictured here.

Popularity of Agility

It is easy to explain why agility has become so popular so quickly. Here are six simple reasons:

1. **Dogs love to work.** Because we love dogs, it makes us happy to see them happy. There is a sense of naturalness about agility. Dogs run, jump, climb, and scramble. Like kids, dogs love having a job and doing it well.

2. **Dogs love to play.** An agility course is the dog equivalent of an amusement park. What could possibly be more fun than thundering through a tunnel or hurdling over a line of jumps?

3. **Agility offers variety.** Unlike some other dog sports, which are somewhat predictable, agility offers endless variety. Because judges design unique agility courses for each trial, no two courses are ever the same. In addition, different organizations offer different games and give them wonderful names like Wild Card, Snooker, and Tunnelers to create a sense of excitement and possibility.

4. **Agility is complex.** This sport requires both dog and handler to learn a wide array of skills. Even the most experienced participants are continuously honing their skills. This keeps agility from getting boring.

5. **Agility allows mixed breeds.** Most organizations that sponsor agility encourage all dog breeds to participate. Historically, many events have been limited to purebred dogs. However, in agility, a Papillon who can trace his ancestry back to Marie Antoinette regularly goes head to head with a terrier who can trace his ancestry back to a street corner in San Francisco.

6. **Agility develops a true partnership.** Agility is a team game. It requires that human and dog become experts at reading each other's body language. The long-term training required is fun and rewarding for both partners. Effective agility training creates a tight bond between partners that transcends that of the typical pet–owner relationship.

Your Canine Partner

Any dog in good health and who likes to run is a good candidate for this sport. As mentioned, some agility organizations, like the AKC, allow only purebreds, but other organizations, such as the North American Dog Agility Council (NADAC), allow mixed breeds.

Agility can provide a great outlet for most dogs. For an active dog looking for a job, agility can help him get adequate physical and mental exercise. For the retiring canine, agility can

Making Agility Even More Fun

In addition to being able to move around the course, other aspects of agility training will enhance the fun for you and your dog. A positive approach to training, discussed in more detail later, is essential. Also, a good sense of humor will take you a long way on those days when you trip and fall over the finish line. Lastly, a generous dose of patience is important during the many months of training required to learn handling skills and to teach your dog the many aspects of agility.

build confidence. The bottom line is that agility is fun for most dogs and for their human partners. Nothing is better than watching your canine pal handle an agility course with speed, precision, and intensity.

Agility Organizations

Although agility may require some travel to trials, plenty of agility events are available for a team that is ready to compete. The agility organizations that sponsor trials each highlight a slightly different aspect of the sport. Each also offers its own titles that are the equivalent of beginner, intermediate, and advanced.

American Kennel Club (AKC)

The AKC offers agility trials for AKC-registered purebred dogs only. The AKC provides challenging courses with course times that allow for a wide variety of breeds to achieve success. The AKC also offers a Preferred Class that allows the dogs to

Agility can provide a great outlet for most dogs.

Laying the Foundation

jump 4 inches (10.2 cm) lower than their normal jump height and allows a bit of extra time to complete the course. Any dog can participate in Preferred, and it is often selected as an option for older dogs who still have the drive to participate at some level.

Canine Performance Events (CPE)

Canine Performance Events (CPE) is a relative newcomer to the list of agility-sanctioning organizations. CPE emphasizes the importance of fun in agility for both pure- and mixed- breed dogs and their handlers. CPE offers five levels of titles and many games. This organization also offers a class with lower jump heights for veteran dogs.

North American Dog Agility Council (NADAC)

NADAC opens its trials to both purebred and mixed-breed dogs. NADAC is known for its

---

Agility on the Internet

Hundreds of websites are devoted to agility. The list includes agility schools, regional clubs, trial dates, agility camps, and national agility organizations.

The following links to the major organizations that sponsor agility will help you begin to explore the wealth of information available. Plan to spend the better part of a rainy afternoon!

AAC
Agility Association of Canada
www.aac.ca
AKC
American Kennel Club
www.akc.org
ASCA
Australian Shepherd Club of America
www.asca.org
CPE
Canine Performance Events
www.K9cpe.com
DOCNA
Dogs on Course in North America
www.docna.com

NADAC
North American Dog Agility Council
www.nadac.com
The Kennel Club
www.the-kennel-club.org.uk
UKC
United Kennel Club
www.ukcdogs.com
USDAA
United States Dog Agility Association
www.usdaa.com

Falling in Love With Agility

flowing, fast courses that are well suited for speedy dogs. NADAC also offers a special class for veteran dogs and veteran handlers that provides lower jumps and longer course times.

United Kennel Club (UKC)

The UKC is open to UKC-registered dogs only. The UKC has the most generous course times of all the agility organizations and also features the lowest jump heights. In addition, it offers a program for exhibitors with disabilities.

United States Dog Agility Association (USDAA)

The USDAA, which welcomes all dogs, promotes agility as a national and international athletic event. USDAA sponsors an annual event in the United States and invites the best competitors from all over the world. It also organizes a team to compete abroad at an annual international event.

The USDAA offers two programs: Championship and Performance. The Championship Program focuses on the highest level of international standards. The Performance Program attracts teams seeking a recreational approach to agility competition or lower jump heights.

Many agility organizations offer both standard and nonstandard classes.

Laying the Foundation

Types of Agility Classes

Each of the agility organizations described offers two types of classes at trials: the Standard agility class, which includes all the agility obstacles, and the Nonstandard class, which includes some of the obstacles, depending on the specific rules of the game. For many competitors, the nonstandard classes often determine which trial to enter when multiple trials are sponsored by different organizations on the same weekend.

Caution

All the instruction presented in this book is important. However, some ideas have a make-it or break-it quality. Throughout the book, watch for a summary of those essential ideas under this heading.

The nonstandard classes, often referred to as *games*, emphasize different types of teamwork from that found in standard classes. For example, in Gamblers, a nonstandard class offered in NADAC and USDAA, teams start the run by making up their own courses, racking up points like a pinball machine. Then the team must demonstrate the dog's ability to complete obstacles at a distance from the handler. In the AKC Jumpers with Weaves, another nonstandard class, teams fly through courses that have only tunnels, jumps, and weave poles. In Snooker, a game offered by USDAA and CPE, teams must race back and forth between designated "red" obstacles and other obstacles. The games are such fun that many handlers confess they find them downright addictive.

How to Begin

Most agility competitors don't own agility obstacles—at least not at the beginning. If you live near a city or town, you will likely find a dog-training club that offers introductory classes, an agility training school, or an agility club. Contact these places and ask about classes.

If you have trouble finding people in your area, look up the national agility organizations on the Internet. Most websites list regional clubs and contact names and provide calendars of agility events. Then, find a trial in your area and attend. The trial secretary can steer you to local agility training schools.

Agility competitors are a very large and tight-knit group. Once you make your first contact, it will be easy to find opportunities to learn how to play this wonderful game.

Falling in Love With Agility

Chapter Two

How the Game Is Played

The point of agility is to show how quickly you and your dog can work as a team to complete a long series of "obstacles." These obstacles are set up in unique patterns by teachers and agility judges to showcase a team's cohesiveness. The main difference between agility and other dog sports is that completion of the course is timed, which encourages speed as well as accuracy.

The Agility Obstacles

As you begin your training, you will encounter a typical set of obstacles. They fall into five groups. Let's become familiar with them, and then I'll show you how they might be positioned to create a typical novice-level course.

Contact Obstacles

Three items are included in this group: A-frame, dogwalk, and teeter. The contacts have earned their name because each of these obstacles has a designated zone that the dog must touch to receive "credit" for performing the obstacle. The contact zones are always

painted a contrasting color from the rest of the obstacle so that it is visible to dog and handler. The contact zones are intended to make the obstacle safe for the dog by slowing him down just a bit or discouraging a wild jump.

A-Frame This obstacle consists of two panels approximately 4 feet (1.22 m) wide, set so that the dog must climb up one side and descend the other. The height of the A-frame varies from 5 feet 6 inches (1.68 m) to 6 feet 3 inches (1.91 m), depending upon the agility organization and the size of the dog. Most A-frames have narrow cross slats to increase a dog's footing.

Dogwalk The dogwalk gives meaning to the old concept of "walking the plank." It consists of a center section elevated between 3 feet (0.91 m) and 4 feet (1.22 m) and a ramp on either end. The entire obstacle is more than 30 feet (9.14 m) in length and 12 inches (0.30 m) wide. Like the A-frame, the dogwalk generally has slats on the incline and decline to help the dog hold on.

Teeter The teeter, or seesaw, bears a marked resemblance to the child's playground toy. It consists of a plank attached to a fulcrum that allows it to rock back and forth. The teeter is also 12 inches (0.30 m) wide. The dog learns to run up the teeter, shift the balance, and run off as the teeter hits the ground.

Above, from top:

The A-frame consists of two panels approximately 4 feet (1.22 m) wide, set so that the dog must climb up one side and descend the other.

The dogwalk consists of a center section elevated between 3 (0.91 m) and 4 feet (1.22 m) in length and a ramp on either end.

The teeter consists of a plank attached to a fulcrum that allows it to rock back and forth.

Caution

Agility training requires a long-term commitment. Getting your dog ready for a trial will take a least a year (and probably more) of regular training. Be careful not to pressure yourself or your dog to learn the game so quickly that it takes the edge off the fun.

Laying the Foundation

Jumps

The lion's share of agility consists of jumps, and you will find them in a multitude of sizes and shapes. You will encounter single bar jumps that test a dog's ability to jump high and spread jumps that test a dog's ability to jump high and wide. The panel jump gives the illusion of being a solid wall. The tire jump consists of a circular object that resembles a tire suspended in a rectangular frame. The broad jump, used only in one venue, is a carryover from the world of competitive obedience.

Jumps can also have wings attached that resemble small sections of fence on either side of the stanchions. The wings add difficulty because they require the handler to work farther away from the dog.

Tunnels

There are two types of tunnels, one used more frequently than the other.

Open Tunnel The open tunnel consists of a tube of flexible material from 15 feet (4.57 m) to 20 feet (6.10 m) in length. It is fastened down to keep it from rolling around. It can be used in a straight or curved direction on an agility course. Multiple open tunnels often are used within a single agility course.

Above right, from top:

The single bar jump tests a dog's ability to jump high.

The spread jump test a dog's ability to jump high and wide.

The tire jump consists of a circular object that resembles a tire suspended in a rectangular frame.

The broad jump, used only in one venue, is the single carryover from competitive obedience.

21

Closed Tunnel This obstacle has a short, rigid opening similar to a barrel with a long, fabric chute attached. It is sometimes referred to as the "chute." Dogs enter through the barrel and then push their way through the flat section of nonslip material.

Weave Poles

This obstacle consists of a series of vertical poles—generally 6 or 12—attached to a fixed base through which dogs must weave without missing a pole. The poles are approximately 20 inches (0.51 m) apart. Fast agility dogs can complete 12 weaves in less than three seconds.

Table

The table is intended to show that a dog is not only fast but can also be controlled. The table, also appropriately called the *pause table*, is 3 feet (0.91 m) square. The height is adjusted for different jump heights. Dogs must leap on the table, either *sit* or *down* (as determined by the judge), and stay in that position for five seconds.

Above, from top:

The open tunnel consists of a tube of flexible material.

The closed tunnel has a short, rigid opening similar to a barrel with a long, fabric chute attached.

The weave poles consists of a series of vertical poles through which dogs must weave without missing a pole.

The table is intended to show that a dog is not only fast, but that he can also be controlled.

Laying the Foundation

From Individual Obstacles to Sequences

The initial emphasis in agility training is on teaching dogs how to perform each of the obstacles quickly and safely. In subsequent chapters, we'll explore that process. This is very important foundation work and takes weeks or months, depending on the difficulty of the specific obstacle. For example, dogs can learn to perform the open tunnel very easily, but the teeter and weaves require several months of methodical training.

Once a dog is comfortable with individual obstacles, he is introduced to performing two obstacles, then three, in sequence. This is, in fact, called *sequencing*. Very slowly, additional obstacles are added, until the dog is able to run a full course. An agility course is simply a longer sequence.

Types of Games

Once your dog enjoys and can perform a series of obstacles, a variety of agility games are possible. In fact, the different games have expanded exponentially in recent years. Let's take a look at a few of the choices you will have.

Standard Agility

This is the meat and potatoes of agility. If you have seen agility on television, this is what you have watched. It will include most of the obstacles we have discussed. At the novice level, the standard courses consist of 13 to 15 obstacles set up to test a dog's ability to perform them safely and with reasonable speed.

Jumpers

Jumpers courses are the drag races of agility. The courses consist of jumps, tunnels, and sometimes weave poles. The emphasis is on speed, with none of the contact obstacles to slow the dogs down.

Gamblers

This game allows a handler to make up her own course in the beginning. Then, when a whistle blows, the handler must direct her dog, from a distance, to perform a short series of obstacles established by the judge.

Pairs

Two teams split an agility course in half, and each run their half. Their scores are combined.

Colors

Two short courses, each designated as a certain color, are intertwined in the same ring. Handlers must pick one course and successfully run it without doing any of the obstacles in the other course.

Sample Standard Novice Course

Each course at an agility trial is unique because it is designed by the judge of the day and cannot be reused in the same area. This standard course highlights the typical challenges at the novice level, although small variations in courses will appear, depending on the sponsoring agility organization.

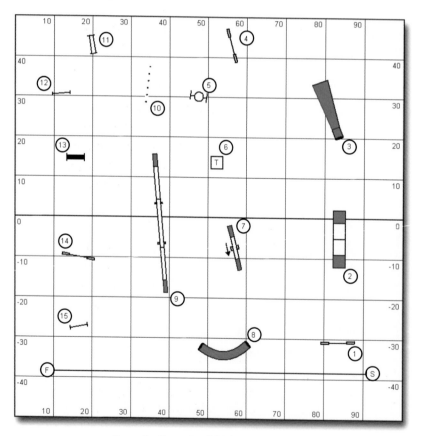

Legend

1 Single-bar jump with wings
2 A-frame
3 Closed tunnel
4 Single-bar jump with wings
5 Tire jump
6 Table
7 Teeter
8 Open tunnel
9 Dogwalk
10 Weaves
11 Spread jump
12 Single-bar jump
13 Panel jump
14 Single-bar jump with wings
15 Single-bar jump

Sample Standard Novice Course

Laying the Foundation

Handling This Sample Course

Now that you have had a chance to learn about the obstacles and to see how an agility course is set up, let's see what it would be like to run the Standard Novice course I've described. Imagine that you have been training your dog to do agility for at least a year. Your dog knows how to perform all the obstacles. You have learned basic handling techniques and know all the rules. You are ready to put it all into action.

Agility Speak

A *lead out* is a strategy in which the handler begins a run on an agility course by walking out ahead of the dog and calling him over the first couple of obstacles.

The day of your first trial finally arrives. It is time for your Novice group to run. The gate steward calls your name, and you walk into the ring with your canine partner.

You put your dog on a *stay* behind the start line. You walk halfway to the A-frame. This is known as a *lead out*, and it is used to get you in a good position to start the course. You release your dog, and as he clears the first jump, you start to run and direct him up the A-frame. As he starts to descend, you give him the *touch* command. He is a good boy, and stops in the correct position with his back feet on the A-frame and his front feet on the grass.

You release him from the contact and send him into the closed tunnel. He dives in, and you race to meet him at the end. Running with him, you send him over the next jump. Then there is a tight turn to the tire, so you turn your shoulders and feet to pull him toward you with your body language. You point at the tire, and he finds it easily.

As soon as he clears the tire, you call him again so that he doesn't

Participating in agility with your dog will help cement your bond.

How the Game Is Played

Agility Speak

When competing in a trial, an agility team is trying to earn a *qualifying score* in each run. The time allowed to complete the course and the number of points required to qualify vary from novice level to excellent level and organization to organization. When a team earns a designated number of qualifying scores, the dog earns a *title* from that organization.

go toward the dogwalk. You run as fast as you can toward the table and give your *table* command. He hops on. He takes a moment before he sits, but once he is seated, he holds it like a rock. The judge counts five seconds aloud. As soon has she says, "Go," you release your dog, with him now on your left side, and take off together toward the teeter.

Your dog races right onto the teeter, and you remember to stay across from his head so that he doesn't jump off. He shifts the balance on the teeter and slams it to the ground. You make him hold that position for just a second to make sure that the judge sees that it is down. You release him and send him to the open tunnel. He lowers his head and races in. You front cross while he is in the tunnel. This means that you turn in a small circle at the end of tunnel so that you can pick him up on your right hand when he exits.

Next, you both take off toward the dogwalk. You slow a bit to help him get on and then stay next to him as he lopes across. Again, you ask him to touch at the bottom of the contact to make sure that he gets at least one foot in the designated contact zone.

After completing your run, be sure to reward your dog.

After releasing him from the dogwalk, you help him find the weave poles by singing the weave pole song, "Go poles, poles, poles." He enters perfectly, and you are pleased to see him snake through the six poles so easily.

Now only the final line of jumps remains. You use your shoulders and feet again to help your dog make the corner from the weaves to the jumps. He follows your body language perfectly and races down the line of jumps ahead of you as you have trained him to do. He crosses the finish line with you just a second behind.

You praise your dog and race for his treat bag set away from the ring. You are both grinning.

Although the point is always to have fun with your dog, you are also excited that you might have qualified on your first try. Your dog performed all the obstacles in the correct order, touched each of the contract zones, and did not knock down any jump bars. When the score sheets are posted a few minutes later, you see your name with a big Q next to it. (Each time you qualify, it counts toward earning an agility title.)

Although there will always be more to learn in the sport of agility, you are pleased that all your training has paid off. There is no doubt in your mind that you will be back to play the game again soon.

Now that you have some familiarity with the agility obstacles, how a typical agility course is set up, and how it might feel to run a course with your dog, we'll spend the rest of this book learning about the sport in more depth. You will learn how to prepare your dog for agility, how to teach each of the obstacles, how to handle your dog, how to enter a trial, and lots, lots more. You are laying a solid foundation for playing the agility game. Let's take the next step on this grand adventure!

How the Game Is Played

Chapter Three

Selecting Your Canine Partner

I f you have decided you want to try agility, you first need to select your canine teammate. Your choice might be as close as the dog lying near your feet. If your current dog does not share your aspirations of racing around an agility field, though, you might want to consider purchasing or rescuing a new dog with agility potential.

The "Right" Dog

Training an agility dog is a lengthy process, so it makes sense to start with a dog who will be fun to train and with whom you can enter competitions for many years. The dog's personality, physical characteristics, and health all play a part in determining whether he will make a good agility partner.

Desirable Personality Traits for an Agility Dog

Dogs come with as many personalities as people. Some have the potential to love agility, and others do not. An honest appraisal of your dog is the first step toward playing the game.

Energy Level Agility is an active sport. Although running a course generally takes less than a minute, an agility dog needs stamina in a number of situations. First, agility classes alone are usually an hour long, minimum. Although dogs take turns practicing the obstacles, your dog needs to be alert and ready to go when his turn comes around. Second, agility trials stretch over entire weekends. Although dogs can nap during the day, they still need to be ready to run at different times during the day. These cautions do not mean that your potential partner needs to be manic; however, if he finds a walk around the block a long outing, and it is not just a lack of conditioning, he may not have what it takes.

Willingness to Run Agility requires that dogs cover ground quickly. For some breeds, such as the German Shepherd Dog and Dalmatian, trotting rather than running is the natural gait. It is challenging but possible to get these breeds to move quickly enough to complete courses in less than the maximum time. You can test for this by playing a game of fetch with your dog. Throw a ball or a Frisbee, and observe whether your dog runs or trots to get it. If your dogs travels at a trot by choice, you will need to spend extra time encouraging him to run.

An agility dog requires stamina.

Laying the Foundation

Interestingly, some dogs who are natural runners, such as the Greyhound, have trouble running through the tight turns of an agility course because of their huge stride.

Interest in Working With You Agility requires dog and human to work closely together, and that requires some interest on the dog's part in working with you. A number of breeds—some very fast hounds, in fact—are rather cat-like. While they certainly love their owners, they don't have much interest in collaborating. The northern breeds, such as Siberian Huskies and Malamutes, also bring a certain independence that is a virtue in a sled dog but can be a challenge in agility, where working together with the handler is essential. This characteristic should not be confused with a dog who has simply not learned yet to be a partner. While outstanding examples exist of excellent agility dogs from virtually every breed, it is a good idea to take an objective look at your dog. A basic obedience class can give you a good sense if your dog wants to participate in agility with you.

Prey Drive Agility involves you and your dog running as a team. Prey drive, the desire to chase a moving object, is lovely in a future agility dog because it guarantees that your dog will want to chase you. A dog who is not excited by your motion is likely to lose interest on an agility course and head off to do his own thing.

Confidence Agility requires a certain degree of confidence. This characteristic is instrumental in learning to perform the obstacles. It also helps a dog adapt to the environment of agility trials, where a great deal of activity and stimulation is present. Not all dogs come to agility with the same degree of confidence and ease with the environment. Although many dogs gain confidence while learning this sport, a few never do.

Trust of People Agility requires that dogs interact with a variety of people. During agility classes, especially in the earlier stages of training, it is important that your teacher or another student be able to restrain your dog while you lead out and call him to you.

A dog who is reluctant to be handled by anyone but you will be difficult to train. In fact, your dog must be willing to accept the proximity of strangers without feeling threatened, because a judge will be in the ring with you while you are competing. Although judges' styles vary, some may come quite close to the dog while he is on the contact equipment or table.

Selecting Your Canine Partner

Positive Interactions With Other Dogs The sport of agility requires that a dog must interact in a positive manner with other dogs. This is important in an agility class, because dogs are turned loose—generally one at a time—to practice an obstacle or sequence. It becomes even more important at agility trials, where dogs are in close proximity throughout the day. When it is your turn to compete, your dog will be loose in the ring with many other dogs nearby. While most behavioral issues can be addressed in agility, aggressiveness is not tolerated because of the danger it presents to other dogs.

Physical Characteristics of an Agility Dog

Any breed or mixed breed can engage in agility. Toy breeds such as the Chihuahua, giant breeds such as the Great Dane, long-backed breeds such as the Dachshund, and short-legged breeds such as the Bassett Hound have all earned agility degrees. Because dogs of different sizes jump different heights, stature is not an issue. In addition, several of the agility organizations allow extra time to run the course to accommodate the shorter stride of smaller breeds. While agility is certainly easier for medium-sized dogs with long legs, you can have fun with most healthy dogs.

Dogs can compete in agility as long as they remain in good health.

Laying the Foundation

Even breeds such as the Bulldog, which may have trouble breathing and are sensitive to the sun, can play the game, but they may require extra, specialized care in training and at trials. If you have questions about the appropriateness of the sport for your individual dog, check with your veterinarian before you start agility.

Agility Speak

Long bones, such as the humerus and femur, grow from the ends at areas called *growth plates*. If the cartilage of these growth plates gets damaged, the bone will stop growing.

Growth plates close for different bones between 6 and 13 months of age, depending on the size and breed of dog. Be careful about any jumping or twisting activities with your puppy before the growth plates close. Once he hits about 1 year of age, you might want to x-ray at least one joint area to confirm that the growth plates have closed.

Conformation As a pet, how a dog is put together is not terribly important. However, once we ask dogs to run, jump, and weave, their skeletal and muscular structure becomes important. It will determine not only how fast they can run, but more importantly, how prone to injuries they might be. It is interesting to note that the conformation required of show dogs and the conformation required of agility dogs are not identical. Conformation shows often allow structure such as straight shoulders or extreme angulation in the hind end that does not translate well into the athletic game of agility.

Ideally, an agility candidate should have a laid-back shoulder, because this structure provides the dog with shock absorbers, and moderate angulation in the hind end, which allows him to drive his hind legs back when running. That said, many high-powered agility dogs, including many Shelties, have straight shoulders. A dog with straight shoulders is like a car without good shock absorbers. Scout, my lively four-year-old Sheltie, falls into this category. Recognizing this structural issue has helped me to modify her training by limiting fast, jarring stops at the bottom of the A-frame that could make her sore or cause an injury.

Another consideration is a breed's general shape. Bassets and other breeds with long backs and short or bowed legs are at higher risk, especially if overweight, of injuring disks in their backs. Grace the Corgi, a young, lightning-fast Pembroke Welsh Corgi who I am training for a friend, fits into this category. I am working to help her stay sound by training at lower jump heights and limiting the number of repetitions during a training session.

Health First, performance dogs must be in good health. They must be free of bone or joint diseases, such as hip dysplasia, and they should be free of parasites. Consult with your

Selecting Your Canine Partner

veterinarian to be sure your dogs receive appropriate vaccinations, since they will be exposed to many other dogs.

Good eyesight is particularly important for the agility dog. It is recommended that you have your puppy or young dog checked to rule out any of the genetic problems that could make jumping unsafe. Then, it is prudent to have the dog checked again at 2 to 3 years of age (5 to 7 in breeds prone to late-onset PRA [Progressive Retinal Atrophy]) and yearly for your veteran dog.

Several organizations allow deaf dogs to participate in agility. Deaf dogs have received titles from CPE, NADAC, UKC, and USDAA.

If purchasing a dog from a breeder, always ask to see health reports on the parents. Responsible breeders expect you to do this.

Age Agility organizations have a minimum age at which dogs can begin competing. Generally, the ages range from 12 to 18 months, although the UKC allows younger pups. One of the most important factors in starting young dogs is the closing of growth plates in the long bones, such as the humerus and femur.

The canine athlete should be lean.

Laying the Foundation

There is no upper end at which dogs must stop competing, as long as they remain in good health. Many dogs have begun their agility careers well into their middle years. Dogs have been known to compete into their teens, which in human years, would make them senior citizens.

Weight Excess weight is obviously a problem for any dog, but it becomes a serious issue with a dog who is being asked to run and jump at top speed. It is simply not healthy for dogs packing extra pounds to work as athletes. Here are a few guidelines to check your dog's weight:

- Feel each rib. The ribs should be *easily* palpable. (We are talking about minimal fat covering here. Be honest.)
- Feel the spine and hips. They should be fairly prominent and easy to find.
- Look at your dog from the top. He should have a clear waistline; that is, there should be a clear indent between his rib cage and hind legs.
- Look at your dog from the side. The abdomen should tuck up toward the hind legs.

If you are planning to start agility, and your dog does not pass this test, talk with your veterinarian about a diet. Often substituting vegetables such as pumpkin and green beans for a portion of your dog's regular food provides a simple fix.

Current Dog or New Dog?

Most people who become involved in agility begin with their existing dog. However, sometimes people acquire a new or second dog with agility in mind.

Getting Started With Your Own Dog

If you have a dog who passes the temperament and health requirements we've just discussed, agility is an excellent idea. Remember, any purebred dog or mixed breed can do agility, but some breeds are easier than others to train for the sport. Dogs with a strong working background and a desire to work with you—notably the herding breeds and some of the retrievers, such as the Golden—take to agility quite naturally. If you attend an agility trial, you will see a large number of Border Collies, Shetland Sheepdogs, Australian Shepherds, and Pembroke Welsh Corgis. Among the smaller breeds, the Papillon and Parson Russell Terrier are also well represented.

As I mentioned, some breeds present a greater training challenge. The Poodle, for example, with his highly developed sense of humor, is renowned for doing the unexpected in the agility

Agility Speak

In agility, dogs are commonly referred to as *high drive* or *low drive*. High-drive dogs are those who bring a lot of energy to the sport and perform consistently at top speed. Virtually all breeds have individuals who are high drive, but the herding breeds are more likely to be high drive than others. Low-drive dogs take a more relaxed approach to the game, although they can compete successfully.

ring. Terriers, naturally, have a strong desire to put their nose on the ground. The bottom line is that some dogs require more patience from the handler and an understanding at the outset that they are likely to do the unexpected in the agility ring.

The way that you approach training will be influenced by your breed. Some high-drive dogs, such as the Border Collie, will repeat an agility exercise until the sun goes down. Other breeds lose their enthusiasm for the game and start to slow down or get bored if they are asked to do something more than once or twice. Although exceptions exist within virtually every breed, you are likely to find that one or two repetitions are plenty for your Beagle, Dalmatian, or Whippet. Some breeds with lots of enthusiasm, such as the Belgian Tervuren and Australian Cattle Dog, can take a strong tone of voice—although good agility training is always positive—while others, notably the toy breeds, lose interest if their handler even scowls. It is important to watch your individual dog's reactions from the beginning and learn what approach keeps him in the game.

Acquiring a Dog With Agility Potential

If your present pooch prefers life as couch potato rather than an athlete, or if he simply doesn't have the temperament for agility, you should look for another dog. You have two options: Purchase a puppy, or adopt a dog from a shelter or rescue organization.

Purchasing a Puppy Step one in purchasing a puppy is to find a reputable and responsible breeder. You can find a breeder in many ways, from kennel websites, to magazine ads, to word-of-mouth. My recommendation is that you visit dog shows or agility trials, where you can check out dogs who appeal to you and talk to their handlers. Naturally, choose a time when they are not preparing to go into the ring. Find out where their dogs are from and how to contact the breeder. Because breeders strive for consistency among their puppies, you have a good chance of getting a puppy who is similar to the dogs you observed.

Litters of puppies from breeders who have a history of placing successful agility dogs are often in great demand. After you contact the breeder, you may need to wait several

Mixed breeds are welcome to compete in agility.

months for a litter. The breeder may want to meet you. Some ask that you write to them about your background in training and how you plan to train the new puppy. A few even ask for references. It is important that you stay in contact during the waiting period so that the breeder knows you are still interested.

A reputable breeder will provide you with the following:

- A contract guaranteeing the puppy's health
- A guarantee that the breeder will take the puppy back under any circumstances
- Health tests such as OFA certification for hip and elbow dysplasia
- CERF (eye) certification.

If you are going to select a puppy with whom you hope to do agility, you will want to look at characteristics different from those you might want for a pet puppy. Three general aspects of the puppy's behavior must be considered:

1. The first consideration is simple. Look for a puppy who is outgoing and not easily startled. Make sure that you are getting a puppy who has been well socialized with

Selecting Your Canine Partner

people from the time he was born.

2. The second category is similar but goes a bit deeper. It is called *pack drive*, and it indicates how much a dog wants to work with a leader. A dog with little pack drive may be overly independent and not much of an agility partner. A puppy with good pack drive will play with the other pups but then break it off to check in with people. Pups with good pack drive are very cognizant of people and have a strong desire to be with them.

Caution

There are lots of up and downs in dog training. Remember that agility is a long-term commitment, and don't get discouraged by any training session that doesn't go perfectly. Just have fun, try it again the next day, and enjoy playing the game with your best friend.

3. A third consideration is something called *prey drive*. Prey drive, a holdover from the days when dogs hunted for their dinner, translates to a puppy who is willing to chase moving objects, tug, and retrieve. These are all characteristics that help a puppy enjoy agility. When you visit the puppies, take small toys to see which ones are interested in following a moving object, playing tug with you and the toy, and bringing it back to you.

Choose a puppy who is outgoing and well socialized.

There are no guarantees when you select a puppy that he will become a top agility dog. Many variables contribute to a dog's performance, but careful selection of your puppy will raise the odds of getting a partner whom you will enjoy.

Adopting a Dog Many good dogs find their way into shelters or breed rescue organizations. If you choose to rescue a dog, you will not only save his life, but you will be providing him with a stimulating life in agility. Be sure to select a dog whom you will enjoy as a pet in addition to his potential to be a top agility dog.

As with the selection of a puppy, you should consider whether an adopted dog will have the right stuff to participate in agility, if that is your goal. The dog should be outgoing, friendly, willing to be handled, and not easily spooked in busy or noisy environments. He should tolerate other dogs nearby and not show any signs of aggression. He should also have an energy level that indicates that he will enjoy running.

In addition, the dog should ideally have a good dose of pack drive and prey drive, which

Indefinite Listing Privilege

If you choose to adopt a dog who has the characteristics of a purebred recognized by the AKC, but who is unregistered, you may apply for registration through the AKC's Indefinite Listing Privilege (ILP) process. By submitting an application, photos, proof of spay/neuter, and a small fee, you may receive an ILP that allows you to participate in many AKC events, including agility. You can find additional details about this process at www.akc.org.

we discussed earlier. When the dog is playing with other dogs or running loose in a fenced yard, does he come back to check in with you? Some dogs who have not been well socialized can be friendly but very aloof. This does not bode well for establishing an agility partnership. If you throw a ball or toy, does he chase it, and even better, return it to you? If the dog has the right traits, it will be easy and fun to learn agility together.

Once you have chosen, purchased, or adopted your agility partner, you are ready to start your work and fun together. It is a journey that will deepen your relationship with your dog to a degree that is hard to imagine. In a few months, you will wonder how you ever lived without agility!

Selecting Your Canine Partner

Chapter Four

Keeping It Positive

In recent years, a massive shift has occurred away from traditional dog training, which is based on correcting undesired behaviors, toward positive dog training, which is based on reinforcing desired behaviors. If you have made this transition, it will be easy to understand the positive nature of training for agility. If you are new to the world of positive training, agility will provide a new approach to dog training.

The Unique Nature of Agility Training

A number of dog sports, such as flyball and lure coursing, require speed. Other sports, such as competitive obedience and freestyle, demand precision. Agility requires both speed and precision. The agility dog must move quickly and respond to your body language to make split-second decisions about which obstacle should be performed next.

It is relatively easy to train a dog to be precise in agility. The challenge is in maintaining a dog's speed through the long training process or getting a dog who is not a naturally fast runner to move a little more quickly. A dog who moves very slowly, strolls through the weave poles, or needs a command before every action is not nearly as much fun as a lively dog who loves the game. Besides, with a slow dog, it becomes difficult to qualify at trials, much less win them, particularly beyond the Starters level, when course times are tighter.

Now that thousands of dogs have been trained to do agility, most handlers agree about what works to train a dog who is both precise and speedy—positive training. Three elements of a positive approach will serve you well as you begin agility training:

- It is correction-free.
- The dog is frequently reinforced for the desired behaviors.
- Communication with the dog is clear, timely, and consistent.

Correction-Free Training

For a dog to play the agility game quickly, he must be relaxed and confident. He must know that you and he are playing a great game together in which games and toys will reward his best effort. He must not worry about disapproval.

Always remember that there are no mistakes in agility. Let's say, for example, that your dog runs into the tunnel instead of taking the jump that you wanted. You have two choices. One, you can use your voice, body language, or facial expression to tell him that it was wrong. On the other hand, you can ignore it, pretend it

Agility requires both speed and precision.

Laying the Foundation

was the right thing, and go on, assuming that you didn't direct the dog clearly enough or that he has not yet learned to read your directions.

A dog who is corrected during agility training, even in the most subtle ways, becomes worried about making mistakes and slows down. This reaction can happen very quickly, and it is very difficult to reverse, so pay close attention here.

The Challenge of Staying Positive

It sounds easy on paper, but in reality, giving no corrections is amazingly difficult. You will want to go, "Ah, ah, ah..." when your dog leaps off an obstacle. You will want to put your hands on your hips when he races into the wrong tunnel. Don't do it.

> ### Agility Speak
> At an agility trial, you will compete in two or more classes, depending on the organization. Each of the classes is referred to as a *run*.

If your dog races over an A-frame that was not "right," pretend it is. Run along and give no hint that you wanted something else. Then, go back and try it again, providing clearer direction for him. If he then gets it, jackpot with a big game or treats.

This approach is more difficult during the novice stage, because you will be learning along with your dog—and you will want to jump up and down and groan when you make a mistake. The problem is that, if your dog is sensitive at all, he will think *he* has done something wrong. With Stanley the Papillon, my first agility dog, I had no idea that my perfectionist behavior was making him careful rather than fast and precise.

I cannot overemphasize the challenge of staying positive. Recently, I was doing a demonstration of agility for a group that was interested in the sport but had never tried it. I had just finished talking about the importance of using positive reinforcement only. Next, I had planned to demonstrate great weave poles with Scout the Sheltie. Incredibly, she balked when I sent her to the poles, and the first thing out of my mouth was a verbal correction. The audience was immensely amused. Old habits die hard!

Positive Reinforcement

During agility training, dogs should be rewarded when they get a behavior right. Since dogs (and people!) repeat behaviors for which they are reinforced, they learn that doing agility is fun and also pays off. Two general strategies are used to reward a dog for playing the agility

Keeping It Positive

game with you—toy play and food. Experienced trainers alternate the use of both of them, depending on the exercise.

Although not all dogs are naturally drawn to toys, most can be taught to enjoy toy play.

Toy Play Toys are a powerful tool for rewarding the behaviors you want in agility. A beloved toy can be tossed over a jump to reward a dog who has driven ahead, or a fast game of tug can reward a dog for racing through a tunnel. In fact, it is much easier to train a dog in agility if he enjoys chasing a toy and interacting with you and the toy.

Many high-level agility trainers spend a great deal of time teaching their pups to play tug and to return a toy that has been tossed, even when distractions are nearby. Not all dogs are naturally drawn to toys, but most dogs can be taught to enjoy toy play. A good strategy to initiate toy play is to combine food with a toy. For example, take a heavy old sock and fill it with a delectable, soft treat. Let the dog sniff it. Then, put it on the floor and move it away from the dog with jerky movements that attract his attention. Move slowly enough so that he can be successful in "catching" the sock. The moment the dog touches or grabs at the sock, open it with a show of excitement and give him a treat from inside. Then, close it up and start again. Gradually, raise your criteria for a treat to grabbing and then chasing the sock.

Food Dog treats are used extensively in agility as rewards, and they are delivered in a variety of ways. You can, of course, simply hand your dog a goodie for leaping on the table obstacle, pushing through the closed tunnel, or coming when you call. A second powerful strategy is to put a treat on a target such as a plastic lid. This will help your dog understand that he is to run to a certain spot. For example, a "baited" target is often set at the bottom of the A-frame to teach a dog where to stop.

Dog trainers are a creative group. A new cottage industry has sprung up of dog toys that are designed to hold food. These products are useful with dogs who don't get excited by traditional toys but who do become wound up about good treats. You can find specially designed canvas bags with pouches for food or cloth Frisbees with a slot that can be packed with something delicious. Agility trainers commonly toss these toys for dogs who don't get excited about chasing a traditional toy; they then deliver a treat out of the pouch after the dog chases it.

Clicker Training

Agility is a complex game, and your dog will learn dozens of behaviors. For your dog to understand exactly what you want, you must communicate with him in a way that is timely and consistent. Fortunately, a wonderful, inexpensive tool exists to do that. If you have not

Caution

Novice trainers generally remember to give treats and play games with their dogs during training sessions. Interestingly, as the dog learns more, handlers sometimes get stingy with reinforcement. Remember to reward your dog frequently, and give him a reason to love the game as much as you do.

already done so, come meet the clicker, a tool that has fundamentally changed our ability to communicate with our dogs.

The clicker is a small noisemaker that tells the dog precisely what he did right to earn reinforcement in the form of food or a game. It is more effective than verbal praise, because the sound is quicker, and it can mark a specific behavior. For example, if you ask your dog to sit, and a well-timed click marks the exact moment the dog's rear hits the ground, it leaves little doubt in the dog's mind what behavior you wanted and whether or not he got it right.

The clicker can be used in agility training to teach a dog to do things like speed up in the weave poles.

Uses of the Clicker

Throughout the book, I will highlight opportunities to use your clicker. If you don't have a clicker, you can substitute a word for the click, such as "yes!" However, it is very difficult to be as precise with your voice as it is with this lovely little tool.

Those of you who are familiar with clicker training know how powerful this little tool is for teaching dogs without resorting to corrections or coercion. For those of you who are just discovering this method, I strongly recommend a class, or if none is available, that you read a complete book about clicker training.

The clicker can be used in dozens of ways in agility. It can be used to teach a dog to run ahead over a jump, to touch the contact zone on the A-frame, to leap onto the table, to speed up in the weave poles, and to stay in the weave poles until the correct exit is reached. It is particularly useful in agility, because it can mark a behavior at a distance. For example, if you are on course and you fall behind your dog, but he leaps up on the table obstacle as you have directed him to do, you can click from wherever you are and then catch up to reinforce the correct behavior.

Three Key Clicker Principles You must remember three important principles in clicker training. First, it is all about timing. Work to perfect your method, so that you click exactly at the moment the dog does what you want. If you click late, the dog will be unsure of what he did to get the reward. Second, once you click, even by mistake, give the dog a treat. You have to deliver reinforcement. If you don't, your dog will come to mistrust the click. Third, confine your use of the clicker to "short" behaviors. For example, it is the perfect tool to teach *sit* or *down* or *jump*, but it is not as useful to teach behaviors that take a few seconds, such as running through a tunnel .

Step 1: Charging the Clicker The first step in using the clicker is to teach the dog that the click means something good is going to happen. Whether working with adults or tiny puppies, just click and treat, click and treat, click and treat. As soon as the dog reliably perks up at the sound, you are ready to move on.

Step 2: Touching a Target Step two is to teach your dog to touch a designated target by using the clicker. A target can be any item you select. For agility purposes, the most useful target is a plastic lid or a clear piece of plastic. Your goal is to have a dog who, when given the *touch* command, will run right to the target, stop, and physically touch it.

Laying the Foundation

Having a dog who will run to a target and touch it with his nose or paws assures a terrific head start for your agility career. The *touch* command will be particularly useful for teaching your dog to stop in the contact zones on the A-frame, dogwalk, and teeter, one of the most challenging aspects of agility training.

Here are the steps to get started:

1. Wave the target near your dog to get his attention.

2. As soon as he investigates the target, click and deliver a treat. Remember the importance of your timing. Click exactly as the dog touches the target.

3. Repeat this many times until he is very reliable about touching the target to earn the reinforcement. Just a note—either a nose touch or a paw touch is okay for future training. Decide which you prefer and reinforce that one only.

> ### Finding a Clicker
> Clickers are an inexpensive item available at many retail pet stores and dog supply websites. Both hand-held clickers and clickers with a band that loops around your wrist or finger are available. The latter is very useful, because you don't have to search your pockets to find it. Buy several, so that you always have one at home and another in your training bag.

4. Next, toss the target on the ground. When your dog touches it, click and treat. You may need to wait a bit until he figures out what you are asking. As soon as he touches, offer him a jackpot in the form of several treats that signal he just did something especially good.

5. When he gets the idea of touching the target on the ground, start using your command just before he touches the target. This will connect the work with the action.

6. When your dog is highly motivated by the game, hold him and put the target down. Give your command and release him to run to the target. When he touches, click and treat. Gradually increase the distance he needs to travel to reach the target.

When you begin to train your dog in agility, be watchful for any loss of enthusiasm or speed. Step back and look at how you are making the game positive and fun for him. You are capable of setting long-term goals for yourself in the sport, but your dog is just out there to play with you.

Keeping It Positive

Chapter Five

Building an Obedience Foundation

Watching a polished agility team on course is like watching a great dance routine. The handler and dog move together as if reading each other's minds. The dog responds to physical cues and verbal commands without a second's hesitation. In fact, when agility is done well, it looks deceptively simple. The truth is that good teams have a solid foundation in obedience and pre-agility training. In this chapter, I'll review obedience preparation for agility, and in the next chapter, I'll suggest other experiences that your dog should have before advancing to agility training. Obedience training and pre-agility work can be undertaken simultaneously.

All of the obedience commands discussed here can be taught to both puppies and adults. Even tiny pups can master a terrific sit and down as long as sessions are kept short. Naturally, only positive methods should be used, and training techniques should be adjusted for the age of your dog.

The Six Essential Commands

A future agility dog must perform six commands reliably, even in a new environment with dozens of distractions. These are *come*, *sit*, *down*, *stay*, *heel*, and a release word of your choosing.

Come (Recall)

In agility, the *come* command or variations of the command, such as "here," are used commonly in two ways: (1) during a run when the handler needs to pull the dog close to her side on the way to the next obstacle, as occurs when the obstacles are set in a curve and the handler is running on the inside of the curve; (2) to call the dog away from the wrong obstacle. In addition, some handlers use the *come* command to rein in a dog who is becoming excessively excited and making up his own course.

***Teaching* Come** If you are starting with a young puppy, here are the steps you should take:
1. Set up a game in which you and a partner call the puppy back and forth in a hallway.
2. Offer the puppy praise and a treat each time he responds to the command.
3. In an open area, play a similar game by tossing the leash back and forth to a partner and calling the puppy. Keep a bowl of low-calorie treats near the door, and use them to reward the puppy for racing into the house when called. It is important not to call the puppy unless you are sure he will come, or he will learn to ignore you. And remember, never chastise the puppy when he comes, even if he was slow or distracted.

If you are starting with an older puppy or dog, here are the steps you should take:
1. Begin with the traditional recall on leash. Have your partner restrain your dog by the collar, and then go to the end of your leash and call your dog. Praise and reward him when he comes to you.
2. When this behavior is reliable, use a longer leash or light rope, so that you can move farther away.
3. Eventually, you should transition to calling the dog off lead. Make sure to do this work in a secure area initially.

For an agility dog, a fast recall is essential, so I would recommend that you not ask the dog to sit in front of you after he comes, as is done in formal obedience training. Rather, I would offer the dog a toy and play a quick game when he comes. The bottom line is that agility handlers must be able to call their dog to them, even when the dogs are very excited.

Gradually add distractions, like other dogs and people, to proof the come command. To accomplish this, I take my young dogs to places with other friendly dogs, such as playgroups or fun matches, and go through the same steps just described. I let my dog's attention wander, and then I call and reward him. If I have trouble getting his attention initially, I put a treat in front of his nose and lure him to me. I make

Caution

Six important obedience commands are important, but the most important one, by far, is the *come* command. It is impossible to participate in agility, a sport in which your dog will ultimately run loose, unless you can keep your dog with you.

coming to me very worth his while by offering high-value treats or a favorite game. I make sure that my dog comes very reliably on lead before I use a long line or release the dog.

Be cautious about calling your dog if there is any danger he won't come, since this will teach him he can ignore the command. Remember that once you start training and competing, your dog must come to you, even when other dogs are running on the training field or in an adjacent ring. You will know he is ready for agility training when he comes directly to you in a setting with other dogs running around.

The *come* command is an essential part of agility training.

Building an Obedience Foundation

Sit and Down

On most agility courses, one of the required obstacles is the table. The dog must jump onto the table, quickly sit or lie down, and remain in that position for five seconds. The judge of the day determines whether the dog will *sit* or *down* for that particular run.

In agility, a dog must do more than respond reliably to a *sit* and *down*. He needs to have mastered a *fast sit* and a *fast down*. A great deal of time can be lost on an agility course if a dog takes several seconds to slide into a *down* or vacillates about whether he will sit. Agility handlers teach their dogs to do these commands with amazing speed.

Teaching **Sit** The *sit* is easy to teach and a great way to practice using your clicker. Here are the steps:

1. Move a piece of food slowly from a dog's nose back over his forehead. As the puppy looks up, his rear will go down. If the puppy backs up to see the treat instead of sitting down, block this motion with a sofa or the wall so that he can't go backward. Don't worry about a verbal command.

2. As soon as his bottom hits the floor, reinforce the behavior with a click or a marker word, such as "yes!" Follow with a treat. Repeat several times over several days.

3. When your dog starts to anticipate the *sit* before you move the food, change the game. Just stand still. The puppy will want to get the treat and will offer the *sit*. Sometimes you have to wait

Dogs need a reliable, fast *sit* and *down*.

Laying the Foundation

uncomfortably long. As soon as he does, click and treat generously.

4. After you have repeated this a number of times, start giving the *sit* command while the dog is on the way to sitting. Again, click and treat.

5. When your puppy is offering the *sit* readily, start to give the command before the action. Don't repeat it. As soon as the pup responds, click and treat.

6. Once the puppy understands the command, start to click and treat the puppy's quickest *sit*. If the pup sits slowly, don't click. Just say kindly, "Oops, let's try that again."

   During this process, do not ask your dog to *stay*. Release your dog or puppy as soon as he sits. The point now is to get a fast *sit* by making this game exciting. Teach the *stay* separately, after the pup has a good *sit*.

> ## Teaching *Lie Down on the Ground*
> Some top dogs appear to lie down or sit before they even settle on the table. It is important to teach these commands on the ground before asking a dog to perform them on the table.

Teaching the Sphinx Down Teaching the *down* command for agility is a bit different from the command used in obedience. The traditional *down* is taught by dragging food slowly from nose to paws after the dog is already sitting. The dog settles onto his front legs and then drops his rear. However, the movement can be performed much more quickly if the dog rocks back and folds his hind end under him. This maneuver is called the *sphinx down* because the dog lies on his legs like the Egyptian sphinx.

The *sphinx down* requires the dog to *down* from a standing position as opposed to downing from a sitting position. If your dog insists on sitting, place one arm under his belly to keep him standing. Using the other hand to lure him with a cookie, start at his nose and drop your hand down in a straight line from his nose to a spot between his legs, close to his chest. To get the cookie, his front end will fold back and down. Take your arm out from under his belly and gently touch his back to encourage him to fold his rear down. As with *sit* training, reinforce the quickest *downs*.

The *Agility Stay*
You can start a run on an agility course in two ways: You can run with the dog from the beginning or walk out ahead of the dog and call him over the first couple of obstacles. The latter strategy is called a *lead out*. Increasingly, agility courses are designed so that a lead out is

Building an Obedience Foundation

The *Sphinx down* is ideal for agility.

an absolute necessity. To be truly competitive, a dog must wait, or stay, reliably at the start line and then respond with intensity when called.

A good *stay* appears fairly easy to achieve in the continuum of training, yet many fine dog trainers have dogs who do not *stay* reliably at the start line. The problem is that all *stays* are not created equal. In obedience training, the *stay* requires inaction on the dog's part. Nothing in front of the dog screams, "Come on and play! What are you waiting for?" In agility, the *stay* is more complex. First, the dog, knowing that the fun is coming, must resist a tremendous temptation to run and jump. Second, the dog must be ready to shift from a *stay* to a run as if he is spring loaded. If he hesitates in performing the first couple obstacles, precious seconds are lost.

The excitement of an agility performance and its need for speed requires that you train the *stay* in an entirely different way, one that teaches the dog maximum self-control. Not only must he remain still despite his excitement, but he must remain keen and ready to respond instantly on command.

Teaching the Agility Stay Many trainers preparing their dogs for agility count on the traditional method of teaching the *stay* command. That is, the trainer sits the dog and corrects him if he changes position. Although the dog learns to stay because of negative experiences, he is never happy or comfortable with the command.

If you have a solid *stay* when you start your agility training, just stick with it. For most dogs, however, it is useful to reteach the *stay* in a way that creates confidence and decreases anxiety. In fact, for agility training, I recommend that you drop the *stay* command altogether. Let's take a look at how this works.

The three-phase method I am going to describe works for both low-drive and high-drive dogs. It is successful because it teaches the dog self-control even when he is excited. It also teaches the dog to remain alert during the *stay*, anticipating that something fun is going to happen. Most important, it communicates that sitting and staying are just an integral part of the game. Here are the steps:

Agility Speak

Treats used to reinforce different behaviors are not created equal. *Low-value treats* are those a dog will eat. *High-value treats* are those that get a dog seriously excited. Dry dog food is generally considered to be a low-value treat, while chicken or hot dogs (or anything your dog loves) is high value. High-value treats should be saved for commands that your dog finds difficult.

1. Using positive reinforcement, teach your dog to sit on cue. If you have been using the words *stay* or *wait*, drop them for the purposes of this *stay* game. The rules of the game are that *sit* means sit until asked to do something else.

2. Start a game with your dog. It needs to be something that requires interaction, such as playing with a tug toy or encouraging your dog to run and romp with you. Do whatever you need to do to get your dog excited and playing with you. While in the midst of play mode, quickly tell the dog to sit. As he sits, instantly click and let him get the toy. If you don't use the clicker, use a marker word such as "*yes!*" and let him play with you immediately. When your dog is doing reliably well at this exercise, move on to Step 3.

3. Play the game as described in Step 2. This time, though, when the dog sits, hesitate a second or two and take a step away before releasing with a click. Engage him in a play reward. Gradually extend the length of time the dog holds his *sit* until he is released, and little by little, increase the number of steps you take away from and around him. The dog is now learning to stay with intensity while you move and to release with drive when given the okay.

If the dog stands up before you release him, tell him neutrally, "I don't think so!" and withhold the toy. Take a moment to collect yourself and your dog. Then restart the game. He will learn that breaking early delays the game. Your dog should make

Building an Obedience Foundation

only the occasional error; if frequent errors occur, you have gone too far and/or too fast in teaching the rules of the game.

4. When he can play the game successfully on the flat—meaning without agility equipment—add a jump to the game. Walk back and forth and around the jump while he stays. Return to him to release and play.

When your puppy's performance is solid, take your *sit* on the road. Practice anywhere safe but where many distractions are present, including other dogs running nearby. Scout the Sheltie and I play this game several times a week at the local park. I get her very excited about chasing her Frisbee. Then I tell her to sit, mark it with a *"yes!"* and throw the toy. Throughout the game, I vary the time she sits before I mark the behavior and hurl the disk. If I forget to practice for several weeks, I always know because she will backslide and break her *stay* at trials.

Heel

Heeling, of course, refers to having the dog walk right next to you on a loose lead. Some top trainers insist that heeling is the basis of all agility, because the dog must be willing to come in close to the handler on some parts of the course and then move ahead on other sections. Other handlers agree that dogs should walk nicely on a leash but argue that extensive heeling work, particularly with lower-drive dogs, creates a Velcro-type dog who is uncomfortable with running ahead on the agility course.

Heeling is a complex topic, and dozens of methods are used for teaching this command. I recommend that you

A solid *stay* is crucial if you want your dog to excel in agility competition.

Laying the Foundation

read at least one book about obedience training for detailed instructions or that you take an obedience class that uses positive training methods. In the meantime, I recommend a middle ground when teaching *heel* that includes teaching a dog how to heel on both sides, as well as teaching him the *let's go* command to minimize pulling on the leash.

Teaching the* Heel *Command on Both Sides To teach your dog to heel on both sides, use different terms, such as *heel* for the left and *side* for the right. Make sure to teach these two commands using positive reinforcement methods so that the dog is not anxious about leaving either position.

The steps for teaching your dog or puppy to heel are as follows:

1. Start with your dog on the left side.
2. Load your left hand with small, soft treats, and hold your leash in your right hand. Your leash should be loose. Your goal is to get your dog to choose to heel because it is rewarding, so don't drag him.
3. Hold your left hand next to your thigh with your palm back.
4. As your dog walks next to you to get treats, dole out small bits of food. Reward every few feet (meters) to keep your dog interested. Only reward your dog when he is in the correct position with his ear next to your leg. If you feed him in different positions, he will get confused.
5. If you are using a clicker, you can click and then treat each time the dog is in the right spot. Otherwise, just mark the behavior with a "yes!" and reinforce with a bit of food.
6. If your dog forges ahead, change the direction you are walking. The leash may tighten at this point, but just keep moving. Your dog will follow you. When he returns to the *heel* position, treat or click and treat.
7. Even when your dog is walking nicely next to you, change direction frequently to encourage him to watch you, and then reward him for walking next to you in the correct position.
8. Gradually, remove the treats from your hand, but continue to treat your dog frequently from your bag.
9. As your dog understands the exercise, follow the same steps and teach your dog to walk in this position (ear to leg) on your right side. (Try using a separate word such as *side*, as suggested earlier.)

Building an Obedience Foundation

10. Once your dog consistently walks by your side, start training in more distracting places. Select challenges that allow your dog to continue to be successful. In new locations, you may need to reward your dog as frequently as you did in the first stage of your training. Later, you can gradually space out the food reinforcement as your dog performs more independently.

11. Because you are training your dog to do agility, you will also want him to be equally comfortable with running on ahead. Some dogs who heel extensively have a difficult time leaving their handler's side. Make sure to spend an equal amount of time teaching your dog the *go on* command that we'll discuss in the next chapter.

Teaching the **Let's Go Command** Teach your dog a *let's go* command. For my dogs, this means that they can go to the end of the leash as long as they don't pull. It does not need to be a formal heel, but you will want a partner who can walk around an agility trial without dragging you.

The *let's go* command doesn't have to be a formal heel, but you want a partner who can walk around an agility trial without dragging you.

Laying the Foundation

Two types of products can help a dog learn the *let's go* command. The first is a head-type halter that keeps most dogs from pulling. The dog stops pulling automatically, because any pressure bends his head back toward the handler. When the handler adds just a bit of reinforcement for walking without pulling, the problem may be solved. However, quite a few dogs don't accept the head halter willingly.

A newer product—a revolutionary redesign of the harness—works easily for most dogs and is easily accepted. This new generation of harnesses connects the leash to a ring on the dog's chest. In addition, the harness applies gentle pressure to the dog's chest and shoulders. If the dog pulls, his own weight turns him around to face the handler. With virtually no formal training, dogs learn in a very short period that pulling doesn't work. These harnesses should ideally be fitted by someone experienced with their use.

Release Word

As in obedience training, you need a word, such as *okay*, that you use to tell your dog when he can move. You will use this command for several purposes on the course. The release word is used to end the stay at the start line, to let the dog know that he can get off the table, and to tell him that he is finished on the contact obstacle.

> ### Alternating *Heel* and *Let's Go*
> Alternate the *heel* and *let's go* commands regularly so that your dog understands that sometimes you want him next to you and other times you want him out ahead.

Teaching the Release Word To teach the release, just say the word you choose, grasp your dog's collar, move forward, and make the dog take a step.

Establishing the Proper Groundwork

You must remember one important thing if you are launching into agility with an adult dog. It is tempting to start agility without laying the proper groundwork. This approach may work at the novice level of competition, where a good *stay* or fast *down* isn't quite as important. Once you are hooked on agility, however, I know you will want to proceed to intermediate and advanced levels. Without adequate obedience training, you may find gaps in your dog's later agility performance. A dog who takes several seconds to lie down on the table or who takes off to visit with the ring crew, for example, can be quite frustrating. Taking the time to lay the foundation for agility pays off in the long run.

Building an Obedience Foundation

Pre-Agility Training

When you visit your first agility trial, you will notice among the hundreds of dogs competing that also many "spectator" dogs and puppies are present. You will see them walking around the trial with their owners, sitting at ringside, and napping in their exercise pens. These future agility stars are engaged in pre-agility training.

Experienced agility handlers know that certain experiences beyond basic obedience directly and positively affect their dogs' ability to be successful in agility. This pre-agility training falls into five categories:

- Socialization
- Learning to play
- Coordination
- *Go on* command
- Reading body language

Socialization: Feeling At Home in the World

Both puppies and adult dogs must be well socialized if they are to enjoy agility. This means that canine candidates for agility training must have enough experience in the world to be comfortable with people, other dogs, and traveling.

As early as possible, puppies must have regular interactions with strangers, a variety of dogs, and different environments so that they grow up relaxed and confident. Consult with your veterinarian about finding the balance between keeping your puppy healthy before his final vaccinations and the need to provide a wide variety of positive interactions and experiences. Well-structured puppy classes provide an excellent opportunity for puppies to play and develop good dog manners.

Dogs should be well socialized if they are to enjoy agility.

Adult dogs who are used to people, as well as puppies, can be prepared for agility by taking them to agility trials for socialization. Make sure the organization sponsoring the trial allows well-behaved dogs on the grounds if they are not competing. If it is okay, take your dog and a chair to a shady place to sit and watch the action. Walk your dog around, but be careful with other dogs, because most competitors discourage casual interactions with unknown dogs. Both Tucker the Papillon, my second agility dog, and Scout the Sheltie virtually grew up at agility trials. By the time they were ready to trial, the routine of the weekend was old hat.

In addition to general socialization, two specific experiences are important for the agility dog—getting used to noise and getting used to crates and exercise pens.

Getting Used to Noise

Agility trials are busy events where your dog will be exposed to many cars, tents and tarps, music, loudspeakers, dog-treat vendors, food stands, and applause. Then there is the teeter obstacle that bangs on the ground and the occasional dog who barks his way through the course. To acclimate your dog to busy and noisy environments, take him to shopping areas, sporting events, and other outdoor activities.

Getting Used to Crates and Exercise Pens

Agility trials extend over an entire weekend. You will want to be free to watch or help at the trial while your dog spends time relaxing in his crate (a small, comfortable enclosure ideally made of wire or cloth mesh for good ventilation) or exercise pen (a wire pen that folds for easy transportation). Puppies and dogs can be taught very early on to enjoy these types of confinement.

It is important that your dog be accustomed to a crate or pen.

From a dog's perspective, a crate is a comfortable, cozy den. Dogs learn to relax in their crate by eating their meals inside, having a good chew on a safe toy, and sleeping there at night. A dog's introduction to the crate should be short—just five or ten minutes. The length of time in the crate can be extended gradually.

It is important for your dog to be used to both crate and pen. Some trials allow crates only when space is limited. On warm days, however, a plastic crate can become quite hot, and your dog will be more comfortable stretched out in an exercise pen.

On your first foray to a trial, set up your exercise pen under a canopy or in the shade. Once you have made sure no escape is possible, practice leaving your dog or puppy for a few minutes, but keep an eye on him from a short distance. Return at regular intervals until you see that he is relaxed.

Learning to Play

All puppies play. However, not all puppies or dogs know how to engage in interactive play with their owner. Learning to play together is very important in agility training for two reasons. First, having a dog who plays allows the handler to reinforce correct behavior in a way that keeps the dog energized. While a treat requires a dog to stop, a quick game of tug keeps a dog moving and excited. In addition, many dogs trained exclusively with treats learn very quickly that you don't have those treats with you when you compete. As a result, they don't perform with the same enthusiasm that they do in practice.

Tug is definitely the game of choice for most agility handlers. When playing tug, it is essential that the handler never pull harder than the dog to avoid hurting the dog's mouth and

The *Drop* Command

Some dogs love to tug, and it is difficult to get the toy away at the end of a lively game. Since you never want to yank a toy out of your dog's mouth, you must teach him a *drop* command. To do this, simply say, "Drop," and offer your dog a high-value treat as a trade for the toy. Gradually, he will understand that letting go of the toy has as big a payoff as holding on.

jaw. Teaching a dog to tug also requires that you teach the *drop* command so that you can bring the game to a conclusion. (See box for more details.)

Other dogs may prefer a toy that can be tossed. The downside to throwing a toy is that your dog might enjoy a game of keep-away rather than interacting with you. One way to retrain this behavior is to keep him on leash as you toss the toy. After he picks it up, gently reel him in. Pet and praise him when he is close, and don't be in a hurry to take the toy.

Many people vehemently insist that their dog will not play. All that this means is that their dog simply doesn't see the benefit of play yet. It is up to you to convince your dog that playing with you is fun. Try squeaky toys, food-stuffed toys (even a food-stuffed sock), and toys on a short rope that you can drag in a way that excites him. Save your dog's favorite toy for training sessions. Be persistent. Teaching a dog to play when he is not naturally playful is an art.

Coordination

Many young or novice dogs are not skilled at managing their back legs. For pet dogs, this is clearly not a problem. However, agility requires that dogs perform the obstacles with a coordinated effort between the front and back legs. Coordination—or lack thereof—is most obvious when dogs jump. Dogs who are just hoping for the best can knock bars off jumps with their back legs, and that is not a good thing in agility.

If your goal is to create a fearless, fast jumper, it is well worth the time to teach your dog to manage all four legs. Agility competitors have designed many exercises to accomplish this goal. Here are my two favorites.

The Ladder Game

Put a ladder, the longer the better, flat on the ground. With your dog on leash, walk him across the ladder. Drop treats on the ground within the rungs to focus his eyes downward. When he steps inside the ladder, reinforce the behavior with praise and treats. When the pup is comfortable, walk him down the length of the ladder, encouraging him to step over the rungs. Make sure to mark and reward the dog's initial movement into the ladder and as he continues to

Find a special toy that appeals to your dog, and use it to help him warm up, to reward great effort, and to keep him energized.

walk within the rungs. He may jump out. If so, make no correction. Just encourage him back into the ladder, or go back to walking across the ladder until he gains confidence. Practice this with the dog on both sides of you. Ideally, you want him to trot through the ladder using front and back legs in a coordinated effort rather than hopping through.

Do this several times each week during early training, and your dog will begin to understand that he must manage his feet or else bang the rungs and sides of the ladder.

Cavaletti

For generations, dressage horses have been walked and trotted over a low line of bars (a cavaletti) to teach balance and confidence in foot placement. Many trainers have adapted this exercise to teach the same skills to their canine agility partners. It is perfect practice for a dog who will soon be walking on obstacles, such as the dogwalk, that are just 12 inches (0.30 m) wide.

To create a dog-sized cavaletti, cut several 4-inch (10.2-cm) PVC pipes in half. Lay them on the ground, cut side down, in a line. Vary the distance between the half pipes. Spacing should be closer for small dogs than it is for big dogs. Walk and then trot the dog over the pipes. Change the distances between them and repeat. Again, encourage the dog to look ahead and to travel at a smooth, easy speed.

If you don't want to cut PVC, you can create a cavaletti by using whole pieces of 1-inch

Pre-Agility Training

(2.54-cm) PVC. Since these will roll, you will need to brace them on either end with sandbags or aluminum cans bent in the middle to keep them from rolling. Later, you can use these as bars on your jumps.

Go On Command

During obedience training, agility handlers emphasize teaching novice dogs to come. While this is important, agility dogs must also be willing to run ahead of the handler when directed. Many times in competition, you will want to send your dog ahead to take an obstacle so that you can get in a good position on course or because your dog can do the job more quickly without you.

The *go on* command can be taught quite simply to dogs of any age. Start by using feeding time to train. Restrain your dog by the collar while you put his food down. Walk back a few feet (meters) and release him. Over the course of many repetitions, move farther and farther back from the bowl and begin using the command. Then, repeat the exercise frequently by sending him to a favorite toy or treat that he has seen you put on the ground. Practice this game in a variety of locations until he is very comfortable racing away from you when directed.

Reading Body Language

Agility, in its simplest form, is a series of tricks performed by a dog upon direction from the handler. Because agility is done at high speed, it requires that the dog react in a split second to the handler's direction. In traditional dog sports, such as competitive obedience, handlers have relied heavily on verbal communication. It is easy to fall into the trap of thinking that agility dogs are following our verbal cues. In reality, though, they follow our body cues, for better or worse, regardless of what words come out of our mouths.

Thus, you will get a great head start in agility if you teach your dog to read your body language. You can accomplish this at home by instructing your dog to perform a series of tricks that emphasize moving as a team. Puppies as young as seven weeks can be introduced to this type of training as long as sessions are positive, appropriately short, and don't put physical stress on their bodies.

Body-language training is easily done in a living room or on a porch. It fits effortlessly into a rainy afternoon or ten minutes before bedtime. There is no doubt in my mind that those handlers and dogs who arrive at a beginners' agility class knowing a few tricks will be

Laying the Foundation

the stars of the class. Why? The dog is familiar with and enthusiastic about learning new tasks and performing them in sequence and under direction. In addition, the handler will have begun developing the skills needed to become a good instructor and team leader.

The following few tricks that my dogs enjoy rely on reading body language. These are also a terrific way for both of you to warm up before starting work on the equipment. If your dog is big enough to saddle, skip those in which the dog runs through your legs.

Caution

Some herding dogs are prone to spinning when they are excited. For example, Scout begins spinning like a top when she sees her dinner bowl. This is a characteristic that you want to discourage, because spinning on the agility course is a terrific time waster.

Avoid situations that stimulate spinning. Scout the Sheltie now goes in her crate until dinner is delivered. Also, don't reward behaviors if your dog spins first. For example, if you tell your dog to sit and he spins first, don't reinforce the behavior by giving him a treat. If he persists in spinning, try putting his leash back on.

Backward and Forward

This first trick is perfect to get your dog moving with you like a great dance partner, which is exactly what you want on the agility course. In this trick, one of you moves back and the other moves forward. Then, you switch roles. Later, on the agility course, you will often want your dog to move toward you or away from you, depending on your body language.

To get started, teach your dog to back up by walking him through a "chute." A chute can be made by placing something such as two picnic benches parallel to each other, leaving just enough width for him to walk through.

Begin by backing through the chute yourself and luring your dog to follow you through. Walk him forward three to five times, by backing up yourself, and reward him while he is inside the chute. Make sure he is comfortable walking forward in the chute before you start working on the *back* command.

Next, surprise your dog by gently walking toward him while both of you are in the chute. Begin by rewarding him for the tiniest movement backward—even a half step. If he gets confused and sits down, try bending over slightly to lower the treat. Next, reward for one full step backward, and then gradually progress to two steps back. Don't expect too much too soon. Once your dog is comfortable backing up, practice walking forward-back, forward-back.

When your dog is good at this game, it is time to transition to backing up without the barriers. To do this, back him up to the end of the chute, and ask him to take a step or two

Pre-Agility Training

Teaching your dog to play games like through your legs and leg weaves is good preparation for the weave poles.

backward without the barrier. Gradually extend this distance. Also, continue to work him inside a chute as you gradually widen the barriers.

Through Your Legs

Teaching your dog this trick is worthwhile because it teaches him to bend himself around a fixed object—your leg in this case. Later, he will need to bend as he weaves through the poles.

To teach the *through* command, bring your right leg forward to make room for your dog, and place your right arm back behind your right thigh. That's the *through* cue. I find that it helps some people to hold the dog's collar with one hand while luring him with food in the other hand. Once you can tell the dog is looking at the food and ready to go through your legs, let go of his collar. (Your dog should be comfortable with collar holding. If not, see box for some tips.)

Leg Weaves

Leg weaves are a great coordination game and a direct prelude to learning the weave poles. Using a treat, lure your dog through from the inside to outside of your leg as you did with the *through* command. Now take another big step with your other leg and lure the dog through that leg from inside to outside. Step with your first leg, and lure your dog through. Vary the number of weaves the dog must do to earn a treat. This trick is a great lead-up to weave poles.

Spin

With your dog standing at your side, get his attention by holding a cookie at his nose. This movement works best if you use the hand closest to the dog to hold the cookie. Make a circle with the cookie to lure him away from you and into a 360-degree spin. He should make a complete circle and end up going the same direction you started. Make sure to teach this trick going both clockwise and counterclockwise. Deliver your treat when the dog has completed the spin. This trick is another good one for teaching flexibility, and done slowly, it is an excellent pre-run warmup for your dog. Be cautious about doing this particular trick with herding dogs who are prone to spinning when they are excited.

Turn

With your dog standing at your side, get his attention by holding a cookie at his nose. Then, draw a half circle to lure him away from you and into a 180-degree turn. Deliver your treat as soon as he is facing the opposite way he started. Make sure to teach this with your dog standing on both your right and your left. Later, this trick will be useful as an agility command, and it will tell your dog that he needs to turn away from you and look for an obstacle.

Close

Close provides a twist to the *heel* command, which you learned in Chapter 5. Typically, dogs heel when you are walking. Agility dogs, on the other hand, must be willing to come to this position and hold it while you are both running. I call this the *close* command.

Teach the *close* command by running in a circle in an open area. Using toys or treats, encourage your dog to race with you on the outside of the circle. He should stay in a position similar to heeling. Reward him generously every lap or two. Make sure to practice running in both directions—and be careful that he doesn't trip you while learning this game.

It is possible to continue your pre-agility training once you begin agility class. However, you will greatly accelerate your dog's progress in agility by getting as much under your belt as you can before going to class for the first time. You will be a star in your agility class if you arrive with a dog who has learned the skills and has had the experiences described in this chapter.

Collar-Holding Tips

During agility training, your teacher or training partner must restrain your dog while you walk the course or practice a handling maneuver. Thus, it is important to teach your dog to accept being held by the collar. To do this, gently grasp your dog's collar and offer a treat. Repeat a number of times. Ask a friend to do the same, and have her reward your dog if he accepts the contact. Practice the same exercise while you walk away.

Agility Speak

The *turn* command is one of several useful directional commands that you need to teach your dog. Turn is used to tell the dog that he must turn away from you and look for an obstacle. Many opportunities occur on agility courses to use the *turn* command, so teaching your dog this command as a simple trick is a great way to introduce him to it.

Chapter Seven

Going to School

I n the early days of agility, people often built a few obstacles in the backyard, and using their intuition and traditional training techniques, taught their dogs how to perform them. Those days are long past.

Today, the range of skills used in agility makes it ideal for potential competitors to work with a good agility teacher. This book is a perfect companion for the other six days a week when you want to practice at home. If you live in an area without access to an agility school, this book will get you well started, but I recommend that you find an occasional agility seminar or camp with experienced teachers to keep your training on track. (More on this later in the chapter.)

As with all types of dog training, it is much easier to teach the dog to perform a behavior correctly at the outset rather than try to retrain it. This is true for people as well. Bad habits in handling, such as using one's arms incorrectly, are much tougher to relearn than to learn correctly from the beginning.

In addition, all teachers are not created equal. If you live in an area with a number of agility instructors, you need to consider several factors as you decide who would be the best match for you and your dog. Before you sign up with anyone, I strongly suggest that you visit potential classes to observe, interview teachers, and talk with other students.

Characteristics of an Effective Agility Teacher

The following are some characteristics of an effective agility teacher.

Competes at a High Level in Agility

You may be a novice, but in the hands of a good teacher, you and your dog will learn quickly. Your teacher should be actively competing at the highest levels in agility in one or more organizations so that she knows the exact skills you will ultimately need to be successful. A teacher who is less experienced will limit your growth.

Puts Safety First

An agility facility should be safe and clean. Dogs should be required to have appropriate vaccinations. The equipment should be well maintained, stable, and dry, because contact equipment can be dangerous when it is wet and slippery. In general, the instructor should make it clear that the health and well-being of the dogs is the top priority.

Adjusts Obstacles

At the beginner's level, it is important to build your dog's confidence on the contact obstacles.

Visit a potential agility class to make sure it is a match for you and your dog.

Laying the Foundation

Novice dogs should start on a low dogwalk, A-frame, and teeter. The A-frame and teeter can generally be adjusted to lower the height, but a "baby" dogwalk is typically a separate piece of equipment.

Requires Dogs to Be Under Control

Agility requires that dogs work while loose in public areas with lots of other dogs in close proximity. This makes it essential that all dogs be under verbal control. Minimally, dogs should know *come, sit, down,* and *stay* prior to beginning agility class. They must also be easily controlled on leash and accept handling by strangers. Most important, potential agility dogs cannot be aggressive at any level, because aggression puts other dogs in the class or at a trial in danger. Effective agility teachers draw the line at including dogs who do not have the required skills and temperament.

Agility Speak

Each agility organization offers a titling program with several levels of difficulty. For example, in USDAA agility, beginners work toward *Starters* titles, intermediate handlers try to earn *Advanced* titles, and experienced handlers compete for *Masters* level titles. Agility teachers should have a track record of successful competition at the highest level in one or more organizations.

Emphasizes Positive Training Techniques

Dogs want to engage in agility only when it is fun. Corrections during agility result in a dog who is either slow because he is afraid of making mistakes, or one who refuses to play the game at all.

An effective teacher will help new handlers focus on positive reinforcement with play and treats from the very first class. She will also discourage the use of verbal corrections that have become habit from other forms of training. Although clicker training is not essential, many trainers help their students to focus on the positive with the use of the click-and-reward technique.

Enjoys Working With Novice Dogs and Handlers

It takes a special teacher to work well with beginners. The first few months of training require patience and a sense of humor on the part of both the teacher and novice handler, as the groundwork is laid for agility. Comic moments will occur as handlers juggle clicker, leash, and treats while trying to get their dog to stop on a contact obstacle. The talented teacher encourages novices, helps them make steady process in acquiring new skills, and creates a fun environment.

Emphasizes the Basics

Tremendous tension accompanies agility. On one hand, there is a definite need to teach dogs basic skills, such as following the handler's body language and touching a target reliably. On the other hand, there is an inherent impatience to *do* the running, jumping, and climbing involved in agility. An effective teacher balances these two needs by teaching the basics while allowing handlers to start simple sequences that are unlikely to scare the novice dog. It is up to the teacher to keep novice handlers from pushing their dogs too quickly to do things such as a full-height teeter.

Novice dogs should begin training on a low A-frame, dogwalk, and teeter.

Individualizes Instruction

Although teachers do their best to cluster handlers and dogs according to their skill level, the reality is that every class will have a range of skills. An effective teacher is able to adjust exercises to meet the needs of different students in the class—for example, allowing one dog who is not quite weaving to run past the weave poles on the way to the tunnel or straightening the tunnel for a dog who is not quite ready to run around a bend.

Communicates Effectively With Students

Teachers, by their job description, must provide feedback to help students. Good agility teachers are able to identify a problem, such as giving commands too late, and then explain how to fix the error in a style that is both clear and encouraging.

Understands how Different Breeds Approach Agility

Dogs come to agility in a variety of sizes, temperaments, energy levels, physical skills, and interest in pleasing their human partner. For example, many herding dogs are genetically programmed to curve back toward their owner rather than running ahead. Teachers who have trained more than one breed themselves, or who have successfully worked with students with different breeds, will be the most helpful in addressing training issues with your dog.

Laying the Foundation

Varies Strategies

An effective teacher not only understands different breeds but is also creative in addressing issues with individual dogs. For example, one small dog who needs to learn to run all the way down the A-frame might respond best to the use of a small PVC hoop that keeps him from launching off partway down. A second small dog with the same problem might respond better to a low jump placed close to the bottom of the A-frame.

Caution

If you have a choice of agility schools, take your time to find a teacher who is encouraging to you and willing to make accommodations for your dog as a unique individual.

Provides a Context for Practice Activities

Most teachers set up interesting practice exercises. The best teachers set up exercises with a theme that they explain to students. For example, the teacher might say, "Today we are going to work on front crosses." This announcement tells students what is important for that class and gives them ample opportunities to practice the skill and gain confidence.

Gives Homework

Attending class once or twice a week is not enough training if one is serious about competing a year or two after beginning. Effective teachers help students continue learning by assigning homework. Early assignments might include teaching your dog to play consistently with a special toy or to touch a target with his nose.

Answers Questions

Agility is a complex activity. It involves training, buying or building equipment, learning about different organizations, sending in entries, and buying travel equipment. Many people come to agility classes without having actually seen an agility trial. As a result, they come in with hundreds of questions. A good beginner's class allows time for those questions, and the wise teacher believes that old saying, "There are no stupid questions."

Suggests Resources

In recent years, many agility products have become available commercially. These include specialized dog toys, treat bags, training videos, and agility magazines. Outstanding teachers make students aware of these resources and where to purchase them. In addition, when students are ready, teachers let students know about practice matches in the region that provide an opportunity to test the dog in a trial-like setting.

Private Instruction Versus Group Instruction

Most teachers offer private lessons as well as group classes. Both offer distinct opportunities for training your dog.

Private Lessons

If your budget allows, private lessons are an excellent way to start your dog. It allows you and the teacher to focus on your pup and determine how he learns best. The lesson can be structured to meet the exact needs of your pup or dog.

Private lessons are also a good idea if you encounter a specific problem with your dog. For example, a dog might have difficulty learning to find the weave pole entry. A private lesson will allow extra time to try different techniques to help the dog grasp the idea of entering the poles from the left side.

There are two disadvantages to a steady diet of private lessons. Generally, they cost twice as much as group lessons. Also, your dog does not learn to wait calmly while other dogs run, a skill your dog will need later at agility trials.

Group Lessons

Learning agility with other handlers and dogs at a similar level is just plain fun. Inevitably, a camaraderie develops with people who share a love of dogs and an interest in mastering a complex sport. In addition, group lessons are considerably less expensive than private lessons. Perhaps most importantly, the group setting provides an opportunity for the dogs to learn to wait calmly for their turn, and when it finally comes, to

Private lessons can be structured for your dog.

Laying the Foundation

focus on the obstacles even when other dogs are in close proximity.

There are disadvantages to learning agility in a class. Understandably, teachers create exercises that most dogs in the class can perform reasonably well. Even when you know your dog is not ready, though, you may be tempted to try the exercise anyway. Doing so may result in your dog becoming nervous about an obstacle or performing it imperfectly. For example, your dog may still need to practice the A-frame set lower than full height. However, if the class is running over the full-height A-frame, it is easiest to just fall in line. Second, it is hard to take as much time as your dog might need on an obstacle when others are waiting. Lastly, some classes are too big. More than five or six dogs and one teacher results in a lot of time spent standing around.

In an ideal world, a mix of group and private lessons is best for novice dogs and handlers. However, many excellent teams have never had a private lesson.

Training With Multiple Teachers

You may be fortunate to live in an area with several agility schools. It may seem far-fetched now, but when you get the agility bug, you may find yourself tempted to take lessons at two different schools. Go for it if you have the time, but keep in mind that teaching agility is far from an exact science. Dozens of different approaches are used in agility training, most of which will work. It is highly unlikely that any two instructors will approach novice instruction exactly the same way. If you are someone who can wade through information and decide what is best for your dog, going to more than one class will accelerate your learning. On the other hand, if you tend to be frustrated by too much information, you might want to stick to one teacher initially, then branch out when you and your dog have acquired the basics.

Agility Seminars and Camps

A growing number of agility camps and seminars are held that allow handlers to immerse themselves in the sport for days. These specialized events allow handlers at a variety of levels to rub elbows and tap the expertise of national and international agility experts. You can find out about these opportunities from your teacher, agility publications, agility e-mail lists, and flyers at agility trials. What could be better than spending a week with friends who share your interest in dog training and the compelling sport of agility?

Part 2
Training for Agility

Chapter Eight

Learning
the Obstacles

Agility training has two distinct components. First, a dog must
learn to perform each of the obstacles separately. Second, a
dog must learn to perform the obstacles in a series, known as
sequencing. Generally, a novice dog learns the easier obstacles,
such as tunnels and jumps, and begins sequencing them while
continuing to master the more difficult obstacles, such as the A-
frame and weave poles.

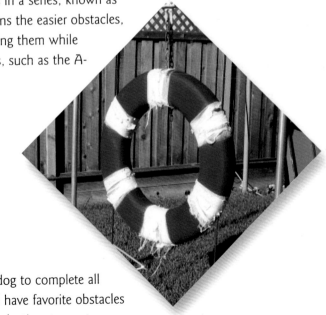

Types of Obstacles

As mentioned in Part I, in agility, the
obstacles can be divided into five groups:

- Jumps (single, double, triple, and tire)
- Tunnels (closed and open)
- Contacts (A-frame, teeter, and dogwalk)
- Table
- Weave poles

It can easily take a year or more to teach a dog to complete all
of these confidently and quickly. Most dogs will have favorite obstacles
that they will learn quickly and others that will take time to master.

On-Leash Work

In your first classes, your dog will likely work on leash the majority of the time. For example, you will run with your dog on leash as the dog climbs a low A-frame or runs across a low dogwalk. This will allow you to guide your dog on and off the equipment. You may sometimes drop the lead while your dog runs through tunnels or through the tire.

Before your first agility class, check with the teacher about outfitting your dog. Most teachers require that you train your dog in a flat collar. Removing tags for class is a good idea, because they can get caught in equipment. Choke collars, prong-type collars, and head halter-type restraints are not used during agility training, although the head halter is okay for walking your dog to class or on the trial grounds. You might find it useful to bring both your regular 6-foot (1.8-m) leash and a shorter tab leash. The tab is useful as a transition from on-leash to off-leash work.

Agility Speak

The *tab* is a very short, light leash that is used as a transition from training the dog on-lead to running the dog loose. The tab makes it easier to catch your dog and to control him while he waits his turn. The tab should be long enough to grasp but not so long that the dog might step on it.

Introduction to the Obstacles

Dogs are capable of learning to perform several obstacles within the same timeframe. A six- or eight-week introductory class typically includes teaching the dogs to:

- Touch a target
- Run through a short open tunnel
- Run through the barrel of the closed tunnel
- Run across a teeter a few inches (centimeters) off the ground
- Run across a low A-frame and dogwalk
- Jump over a low jump
- Jump through the tire
- Get on the table
- Run through the channel weaves

An introductory class may also include some basic sequencing, such as a tunnel and jump, and an introduction to contact work on the three contact obstacles.

During this introduction, your priority should be to ensure that your dog has fun trying each obstacle and that he gains confidence in playing the game. If your dog gets scared by a slip, it is harder to fix than making sure from the outset that the experience is positive.

Remember, no corrections are used in agility. If you correct a dog verbally for any behavior, he will become careful about what he does. A careful dog is a slow agility dog. Your goal is to train a dog who does not know mistakes can be made in agility.

Working With a Partner

One of the many advantages of attending an agility class is that the teacher will work as a partner. Your teacher may deliver a treat as your dog runs through a tunnel, help hold the baby teeter, and hold your dog as you call him over a series of jumps.

If you practice at home between classes, try to get a helper during the first months of training. Perhaps you can find a friend with a dog and alternate working your dogs. In subsequent chapters, I will assume in a number of places that you have help. Eventually, you will be able to work alone with your dog, although it is always fun to train with a pal.

Caution

Sometimes highly competitive trainers who bring their Type A personality to agility want to push their dogs to perform the obstacles too quickly. With visions of trials dancing in their heads, they ask dogs to jump too high, run through long tunnels too soon, or put them on the high equipment before the low equipment has been mastered. Relax and have fun with each part of the training. Your basic training is an investment in a partnership that will last for years.

Knowing When to Say When

There may be times during your training when your dog does not understand what you want. For example, when you are teaching the weave poles, your dog may pop out before the last pole. You may want to repeat the exercise to see if your dog can get it right. If the second effort doesn't improve, don't let your dog keep failing. Make an adjustment in your training to help your dog get the exercise right. In this case, you might put your weave pole wires back on. If you can't think of what to do on the spot, take some time to problem-solve and come back to the challenge on another day.

Practicing at Home

Most of us cannot accommodate a full agility course in the backyard. Nevertheless, I recommend that you buy a set of weave poles and a tunnel and build a table and a few jumps. (Please see Appendix I for instructions on how to build these and other obstacles.)

Basic agility training is best done with a partner.

83

Learning the Obstacles

Chapter Nine

Teaching the Jumps

Jumping is at the heart of agility. In fact, jumps of several different types represent the majority of obstacles that you will encounter on a standard agility course. In addition, all agility organizations offer a class called *Jumpers*, which consists of a course with jumps and an occasional tunnel or set of weave poles thrown in.

Most dogs, of course, love to run and jump, so once your dog has acquired the basic skills, you can play an endless array of jumping games on your lawn or in the park. I can make Scout the Sheltie and Tucker the Papillon incredibly happy by taking them to the park with three or four jumps and their toys.

The Mark of Success

It is helpful to picture the ultimate performance that you want from your dog. Having a clear "destination" makes it easier to train sequentially and adjust your training as necessary.

Purchasing Jumps

If you want to practice agility at home, you need three or four single-bar jumps. Fortunately, jumps are the least expensive of the agility equipment to buy and the easiest to build. (See Appendix I for specific instructions.) This does not include the tire, which is a more specialized piece of equipment.

Two types of jump construction are used. Jumps made from PVC are very reasonable and suffice for light use. However, they do fall over and come apart if a dog hits them hard. The second option is to buy professional-quality jumps that have a metal base and stanchions and a PVC jump bar. These hold up to any use, but the cost is triple that of a PVC jump. You will find dozens of companies that sell and ship jumps if you try an Internet search for "agility jumps."

To be an accomplished jumper, your dog must:

- Jump with speed
- Clear the jump without knocking the bar
- Not waste time jumping too high
- Take the jump from any angle
- Run ahead of you to take jumps as directed

Accomplished jumpers are fast and can easily clear the bar.

Training for Agility

Types of Jumps

There are basically four types of jumps.

1. Single jumps

These require dogs to clear a single bar or a panel constructed of boards to resemble a solid wall.

2. Spread jumps

These include the double and triple jumps that require a dog to jump wide as well as high.

3. Broad Jump

The broad jump, a carryover from the obedience ring, is technically a spread jump because it requires dogs to jump across several boards with spaces between them without stepping on or between them. The broad jump requires a different form of training, because dogs have to jump flat and wide, rather than a simple up and over, and they see little reason not to step on the boards. Because of this, I have separated the instructions for teaching this jump from the other spread-type jumps.

4. Tire

This jump is a tire-like hoop, suspended in a frame with elastic cords, through which the dog must jump.

Jump Heights

Jumping initially should be taught with the jumps set quite low. As mentioned, puppies can be injured if they jump before their growth plates have closed. For young puppies and toy breeds, bars can be laid directly on the ground for basic jump training. For adolescent puppies, jumps should remain below the dog's elbow or lower.

Above, from top:

The single jump requires dogs to clear a single bar or a panel of boards that resembles a wall.

The tire jump is suspended in a frame with elastic cords.

Teaching the Jumps

Winging It

One variation you will encounter is the addition of "wings" to the sides of some jumps. Traditionally, wings look like a short section of picket fence set against both stanchions of a jump. Some agility clubs get creative with wings, using plywood cutouts of dogs or fire hydrants. Wings can add a challenge to a novice dog because they keep the handler from "hugging" the jump (running up to a jump with the dog in a *heel* or side position). Before competing, handlers and dogs should become comfortable with both winged and wingless jumps.

Even mature adults should begin by jumping low. In fact, it is good to vary the height that a dog jumps during training throughout his career. On days when the dog will be asked to take a lot of jumps, it is reasonable and kind to lower the bars one or two notches. Whenever a dog is struggling with a jumping exercise, lower the jumps to make the game more inviting.

Obstacle Commands

When running an agility course, you, as the handler, will direct the dog to each obstacle. Thus, you must decide what word to use for each piece of equipment. Some handlers use different terms to indicate a single bar, a spread jump, or a broad jump. Others do not.

Here are some common commands used by handlers for the jumps:

Single-bar jump or panel jump: *Jump, Over, Hup*

Spread jump: *Jump, Over, Big Over*

Broad jump: *Jump, Over, Big Over*

Tire: *Tire, Hoop*

The words you choose do not matter to your dog. Just pick something you like that does not sound like any other commands or your dog's name.

Steps for Teaching Single-Bar Jumps and Panel Jumps

The process for teaching jumps follows three sequential steps. Phase 1 taps into the dog's innate desire to come to you if you are headed away. Phase 2 teaches the dog to run with you. Phase 3 encourages him to move ahead and jump when directed. This final phase is very important—you want to train a dog who is not limited by your own speed.

During each of the steps below, repeat the exercises until your dog is comfortable, but not

Training for Agility

so many times that your dog gets bored. Smart dogs grasp ideas quickly! Repeating something four times instead of two with Stanley the Papillon didn't make his performance better; it made him slow and grumpy.

If the possibility exists that your dog will take off for a recreational run during your training session, leave the leash on throughout the exercises, but manage it carefully so that it doesn't hook on the jump stanchions.

Jumping Young Dogs

The recommended standard for jumping has been that dogs less than a year old should not jump higher than their elbow. Some veterinarians now suggest that dogs not jump until their growth plates close. A general guide is that dogs with adult weights estimated at less than 50 lbs (22.7 kgs) will have closures by 9 to 12 months, while breeds with adult weights estimated at more than 50 lbs (22.7 kgs) will have closures at 10 to 14 months.

Phase 1: Recall

The easiest way to begin jumping with no stress on your dog is to simply call him over a jump. The dog wants to get to you, and the jump simply happens to be on that path.

1. With your dog on the leash, walk over a low jump together.
2. Next, have your partner hold your dog by the collar behind the jump.
3. Walk out past the jump, giving your dog enough room to land comfortably and take a couple of strides.
4. Face away from your dog, but rotate your upper body to look back at him.
5. Hold a toy or treat in the hand closest to your dog and your clicker in the other hand.
6. Call your dog using a command such as "*Come, over.*" The *come* command pulls the dog to you, and the *over* command tells the dog to jump.
7. Your partner should release the dog and flip the leash to keep it from hooking the jump.
8. Click or use your marker word at the exact moment when the dog is between the jump stanchions.
9. Deliver your toy or treat to reinforce your dog.
10. Repeat by having your dog come to your other hand. For example, if you started by calling your dog to your left

Caution

Your dog should always learn to jump with the jumps set very low. Once he understands jumping, the height can be raised gradually. However, even when your dog is jumping at full height, it is a good idea to alternate heights, practicing regularly at a lower height to keep your dog sound. Scout the Sheltie practices at 8 (20.3 cm) or 12 inches (30.5) regularly. I only put the jumps to 16 inches (40.6 cm) the week before a USDAA trial, and I lower them the day after.

Teaching the Jumps

hand, now look back over your right shoulder, and call your dog to your right hand. Deliver your treat from the right hand. Eventually, you want your dog to understand that he should pay attention to whichever hand you are holding down. This allows you to communicate with him on course.

If your puppy runs around the jump, make no correction. Just put him a bit closer to the jump and move a bit closer on your side to cut down the room for error. If he still does not get it, walk over the jump with him a few more times and then try it again.

Phase 2: Run With Your Dog

The purpose of this second phase is to teach your dog to run along with you and take the jumps in his path, as he will need to do on an agility course.

1. Have your training partner go to the far side of the jump, and put a toy or treat on a target on the ground a few feet (meters) beyond the jump. Let your dog see the target; it can have either food or a toy on it. I am assuming that your dog has been target trained, as described in Chapter 4, and is eager to run to the target, knowing that he will get a reward. The target gives him a reason to run forward and jump now that you are no longer calling him.
2. Position your dog behind the jump. Use your agility *sit* command (see Chapter 5) if he will stay, or hold him by the collar if necessary.
3. Face the direction your dog will be jumping but off to the side, giving yourself enough room to run around the jump stanchion. This is known as a *lateral position*.
4. Make sure your dog is looking at the jump.
5. Release your dog. Use a bowling motion with your hand closest to the dog to show the dog the jump.
6. As your dog jumps, move forward parallel to your dog's path.
7. Click or mark as your dog is in the air over the jump.
8. After he jumps, let him eat the food or play with the toy by the target.
9. If your puppy runs around the jump, your partner should quickly pick up the target and food before he gets it. Remember not to admonish your dog. He simply doesn't see yet why he should jump when he can go around. Put the jump at a lower height. Take him back behind the jump and make sure he sees the target before you turn him loose.
10. If your dog is successful in taking the jump, run out and celebrate. Give him several

more treats on the target or play a spirited game of tug.

11. Repeat the exercise with him on your other side.

If your dog runs around the jump, you can try several things. Make a big deal about putting his treat down on the far side of the jump so that he sees it and gets excited. You can do this by holding his collar and walking him over to see the treat, then walking him back to the far side. Rev him up with your voice, "Are you ready? Ready. Ready." Then, let him go and run with him. Or your partner can bring the treat to her side, show it to him, and step over the jump to return it to the landing side. In either case, it is highly likely that he will jump. If not, the jump may be set too high. Drop the bar or lay it on the ground inside the stanchions and try again.

Phase 3: Send On

Beginner dogs can easily become dependent on their handler's proximity to perform the obstacles. "Velcro dogs" cling to their handlers and are rarely very fast because they have to be escorted to each obstacle. This situation can be avoided if, early in training, you teach your dog to "send" to obstacles from a distance of 10 feet (3.0 m) or more. A good agility dog should be actively looking for obstacles to perform.

Above, from top:

First, call your dog over the jump.

Next, run with your dog.

Finally, send your dog over the jump.

Agility Speak
The term *lateral* indicates that the handler is even with her dog but several feet (meters) off to the side. This is an important position for a handler, because it allows her to avoid clipping the obstacles and also puts her in a position to change sides when needed.

To teach a "send" to a jump, set the bar very low, or lay the bar on the ground. Then, proceed as follows:

1. Send your dog over the jump using a command and arm motion. If you have taught a *go on* command (see Chapter 6), use it. Your command would be, "Go on over," which means "run ahead and then jump." If you have not taught the *go on* command, toss your toy or a bag with food over the jump. Release your dog while the toy is in the air, telling him to "go on over."

2. Click or verbally reinforce the dog as his body travels between the jump stanchions.

3. Follow your dog out to the place the toy or food bag landed after your dog has reached the reward. Don't move so quickly that you are once again running with him. Play or treat there. Repeat this exercise many times until your dog is eagerly jumping out ahead of you.

4. When your dog comfortably goes over the jump after the reinforcement, up the ante. Place the toy or food bag on the ground on the far side of the jump so that he sees it. Jazz him up with your voice while holding him by the collar. Release him to go get it. Click while he is jumping.

5. Run out to play or treat after he has reached the reward.

6. Fade the toy or food bag by setting it out on the far side of the jump sometimes and not other times. Every time you send your dog, follow him out past the obstacle, and play or treat to reinforce the behavior. When the toy or food bag is not on the ground, have it readily available in your back pocket.

Bar Knocking

The issue of knocking bars off jumps deserves additional attention. At an agility trial, dislodging a bar off a jump results in either a deduction of points or a nonqualifying run, which means that no credit is earned toward an agility title. At any given agility trial, dozens of otherwise spectacular qualifying runs are derailed when a bar comes down.

If your dog shows any propensity to knock down bars, read the section on jumping in Chapter 17, "Training Challenges." Diagnose the problem and retrain quickly before it becomes a habit for your dog.

Training for Agility

Phase Four: Adding Jumps

Repeat the first three phases, adding a second and then a third jump. For example, recall your dog over two jumps and then three. This is the beginning of sequencing in agility, in which dogs perform a series of obstacles.

Phase Five: Adding Angles

In the early phase of training, dogs should approach the jumps head on. However, in agility, dogs must frequently jump at an angle depending on the positioning of the previous or next obstacle. Practice asking your dog to jump diagonally by calling, running with, and sending him over increasingly difficult angles.

Steps for Teaching the Spread Jumps

The double and triple jumps should be taught after the dog is comfortable with the single-bar jump. It is important that these more difficult jumps be set at their lowest height for novice dogs and then gradually raised as they gain experience and mature physically.

That said, the steps for teaching the spread jumps are the same as those for single-bar jumps.

Practice asking your dog to jump diagonally by calling, running with, and sending him over increasingly difficult angles.

Teaching the Jumps

Steps for Teaching the Broad Jump

This jump is a carryover from obedience. It consists of several boards, either 6 inches (15.2 cm) or 8 inches (20.3 cm) wide, raised slightly on one side and placed several inches (centimeters) apart on the ground. Unlike other jumps that dogs recognize quickly, the broad jump may not look like a jump to your dog. He may run across or spring off the boards initially.

To help the dog understand the broad jump, tip the boards up on their edges. When your dog jumps these, tip only the first board. When he is doing well with this cue, put the boards flat, but lay a piece of fine wire mesh over them. This helps the dog recognize that the obstacle is a jump because it looks more solid than just the boards, and it is also unpleasant to step on. That said, follow exactly the same process you used to teach the bar jump: recall, run with, and send on. Take your time at each step to make sure your dog knows what you want before you ask for more.

Steps for Teaching the Tire

The tire jump is a circular jump suspended within a framework made of wood, metal, or plastic pipe. The tire is difficult for some novice dogs because they see the space around or under the tire more clearly than the tire itself, and they don't see any reason for jumping when they can run right through.

Several techniques can help the dog with this jump. First, start with the tire at its lowest height to cut off the opportunity for the dog to duck under the tire. Next, as you recall your dog through the tire—Phase 1 for teaching a new jump—bend down far enough so that your dog can see your face through the tire. Then call. If he still wants to go around, try holding your leash through the tire to support him coming through. If he gets nervous, however, make sure not to get in a tug-of-war to pull him through. Instead, use toys and treats to lure him to jump. When successful, offer lots of positive reinforcement in the form of treats or toy play. When your dog is jumping through the tire comfortably on a recall, move to Phases 2 and 3 described earlier.

From Leash to Tab

It is much easier to manage your dog in agility without the leash on. As soon as you know that you can keep your dog from running off or visiting other dogs in class, trade your leash for a short tab. It is an excellent transitional tool between dog on leash and dog off leash.

Training for Agility

It's Just a Game

From the first day of agility training, communicate to your dog through your voice and body language that agility is the most fun you could ever have together. Be careful about getting so serious about agility that it ruins the fun. You may care about doing things perfectly, but your dog is just out there having fun with you.

Occasionally, dogs have brief setbacks when learning the tire. When the dog is consistently successful and you raise the tire, you may find that he wants to take shortcuts around the hoop again. If so, you may need to block the opening with something, such as a board, until he understands this part of his job.

Full Jump Heights

When your dog is comfortable with jumping and old enough to jump at full height safely, you must estimate his competitive jump height. A dog may measure at one height in one agility organization and at another height in a different organization, because the organizations operate under completely different sets of rules. For example, Scout the Sheltie jumps 12 inches (30.5 cm) in AKC trials and 16 inches (40.6 cm) in USDAA. Dogs have little trouble adjusting to this change.

To get a rough estimate of your dog's height, put a ruler (for a small dog) or yardstick (for a big dog) next to your dog's shoulder. Lay a thin, flat item such as another ruler across your dog's withers, and mark where it hits your measuring stick.

Next, visit the website of one or more of the agility organizations. In the rules, you will find a section indicating the jump heights for each dog by height and class. Considerable variation exists between organizations. For example, a dog who measures 14 inches (35.6 cm) at the withers might jump 12 inches (30.5 cm) in NADAC and the AKC in the Standard classes. The same dog would jump 16 inches (40.6 cm) in Championship classes in USDAA.

Agility Speak

The *withers* are formed where the dog's shoulder blades almost come together. You will find your dog's withers just a bit beyond the base of his neck. Dogs are measured directly over the withers to determine their jump height.

When you enter a trial, a judge will officially measure your dog. In the meantime, your estimate will be adequate for setting jumps in training sessions.

Teaching the Jumps

Chapter Ten

Teaching the Tunnels

Of all the agility obstacles, dogs love open tunnels most. Tunnels allow dogs to simply cut loose and run. In fact, many dogs get so ecstatic that they bank up the side of the tunnel as they tear through. Dogs and puppies of any age can start to learn tunnels from their first day in agility training.

Teaching dogs to run through open tunnels is one of the easier parts of training in agility for all but the largest dogs. The giant breeds must learn to hunch a bit to get through, but even big dogs learn to manage it. Training the closed tunnel—also known as the chute—takes a bit more time and patience, because dogs must assertively push through a 12- to 15-foot (3.7- to 4.6-m) tube of medium-weight opaque material.

When you place the tunnel in your yard, strap it down on both ends to prevent it from rolling while the dog is inside. Tie-downs are available commercially. Alternatively, you can stabilize your tunnel by running bungee cords over the top and attaching them to sandbags or heavy plastic water-filled containers on

Purchasing a Tunnel

If you are purchasing just a few agility items for your backyard (prior to selling everything and moving to the country), an open tunnel is an essential item. This type of tunnel is a piece of heavy-duty, wire-reinforced tubing between 10 feet (3.0 m) and 20 feet (6.1 m) in length.

You will find several companies that sell and ship tunnels with an Internet search for "agility tunnel." Big dogs need a competition tunnel that is adequately heavy and durable. For smaller dogs, lightweight tunnels are available; these are convenient if you plan to transport the tunnel to the park.

each side. For large dogs, avoid using inflexible tie-downs such as chain, because it can bruise the spine.

The Mark of Success

No mystery here—a dog has mastered this obstacle when he simply thunders through the tunnel. It is useful to train a dog to send to a tunnel from a distance as great as 10 feet (3.0 m).

One other aspect of performing the tunnel that deserves consideration is what happens when your dog exits. Remember that your dog does not know where you are when he comes out of the tunnel. Dogs are often disoriented when they re-emerge into the sunlight. You can help your dog by talking to him while he is still in the tunnel but close to the end. By hearing your voice, he will be able to find you easily when he runs out. If you wait until he emerges from the tunnel to tell him what to do next, you'll find that he spins like a top trying to locate you.

Tunnels should be strapped down.

Types of Tunnels

Two types of tunnels are used: the open tunnel and closed tunnel, or chute.

Open Tunnel

These require dogs to run through a 15- (4.6-m) to 20-foot-long (6.1-m) tunnel that is either straight or curved.

Closed Tunnel (Chute)

This obstacle requires dogs to enter through a short, barrel-like section and then push their way through a flat section of nonslip material.

Obstacle Commands

Before you begin, think about the command words you will be using. Some trainers use the same word for the open and closed tunnel. Most, however, use two different words, because the performance is different for the dog. The most common commands for the open tunnel are *tunnel* or *get in*. The most common command for the closed tunnel is *chute*.

Agility Speak

The names *closed tunnel* and *chute* are used interchangeably to describe the type of tunnel that requires a dog to push through.

Steps for Teaching the Open Tunnels

Remember to stand on both sides of your dog when practicing the tunnel, just as you did with the jumps. When you start doing full-length courses, you want your dog to be equally comfortable working on either side of you, because you don't know exactly how obstacles will be positioned on an agility course. As with the jumps, three steps are used.

Because dogs are often disoriented when they re-emerge into the sunlight, you should talk to him when he is close to the end of the tunnel, as hearing your voice will help him find you easily.

Phase 1: Recall

The easiest way to get started with the tunnel is to tap into your dog's desire to run to you. In this case, the dog must run through the tunnel to "find" you.

1. Scrunch the tunnel up so that it is short and straight.
2. Have a friend hold your dog by the collar. You can remove the leash or let it drag.
3. Go to the other end of the tunnel. Crouch down so that your dog can see you, and call him. Have a toy or treat in hand to reward him when he comes through.
4. If your dog is nervous, crawl into the tunnel a bit to encourage him. No one ever said agility was glamorous. You might also have your helper toss the leash to you through the tunnel so that you can exert a tiny bit of pressure.
5. Be patient. Take your time to let your dog know what you want. Even Great Danes and Russian Wolfhounds can get through the open tunnel. Never push or force the dog into the tunnel in any way.

Phase 2: Run With

As with every obstacle, you want to teach your dog to perform it while you sprint alongside. This phase gets your dog comfortable with your movement while he dives into the tunnel.

1. Keep the tunnel short and straight.
2. Hold your dog by the collar.
3. Have your friend at the far end put food on a target or drop a favorite toy. Let your dog see the reward through the tunnel.
4. Release your dog.
5. With the hand closest to the dog, use a bowling motion to show him where to go.
6. If your dog runs around the tunnel, your partner at the other end should pick up the treat or toy before he gets it. If he runs through, he gets the treat on the target or a game with the toy.
7. Run as quickly as possible along the tunnel to meet your dog at the far end. Reinforce correct behavior with an extra treat or two, and play with your dog.

Phase 3: Send On

One simple fact is that dogs run much faster than most people. If you are like me, you

Caution

It's a good idea to teach your dog to run past an open tunnel when called. Dogs can become obsessed with this obstacle and will choose it whenever it catches their eye, unless they are taught that it is not always the correct choice.

To teach your dog to run past a tunnel entry, he must know that when you say his name, it means "look at me." If he doesn't understand that, go back and reinforce that behavior with your obedience work. If he does know that he should look at you, and if he is comfortable with running through the tunnel, it is time to teach this behavior. Here are the steps:

1. Set up one jump facing a straight or curved tunnel. Put them 15 (4.6 m) to 20 feet (6.1 m) apart.
2. Send your dog over the jump, but as he lands, call his name so that he looks at you. If he does, offer him a treat or a game.
3. If he plows into the tunnel without looking back when you say his name, you will need to help him out. As he clears the jump, turn back toward the jump rather than face the tunnel. Say his name and give the *come* command as you rotate.
4. When he comes back to you, deliver a treat or offer a tug toy from the hand closest to him. Repeat this several times, so that coming back to you has as big a payoff as running through the tunnel.
5. Start to alternate sending him in the tunnel and calling him away from the tunnel.
6. Gradually move the jump closer to the tunnel until it is 10 feet (3.0 m) away. Always stay at a distance until your dog is successful with that level of challenge.

When the dog is comfortable with these exercises, gradually lengthen the tunnel by increments. Then, gradually curve the tunnel. Remember to practice sending your dog to the tunnel from farther and farther back.

don't want to limit your dog's speed to your speed. Teaching your dog to send ahead and run through a tunnel gives you a chance to catch up. This exercise begins to teach the dog that it is okay if he goes on ahead.

1. Keep the tunnel short and straight.
2. Send your dog into the tunnel using your *go on* command and arm motion.
3. Once your dog is committed to going into the tunnel, slow down so that he gets ahead of you.

Teaching the Tunnels

4. As your dog nears the end of the tunnel, throw his toy, food bag, or a big treat so he sees it as he emerges. Your timing is really important here. He should see the reward immediately and charge forward to get it.

5. Take just a moment, and then run out and play with your dog, or open the food bag and deliver a treat where the bag landed.

Steps for Teaching the Closed Tunnels (Chutes)

The closed tunnel consists of a rigid entry like a barrel and an attached tube of material that the dog must push through. As mentioned, teaching this obstacle takes more time because the dog must learn to push through the dark chute. Small dogs have to learn to push especially hard if the material is damp and heavy. Patience is important on the handler's part so that the dog does not get spooked.

It is important that the dog never get tangled in the chute. Remember to straighten the chute regularly so that it lays flat. If your dog does become tangled, help him out quickly and then do an easier version of the tunnel to rebuild his confidence.

Phase One: Recall

You get the drill. Because running to you should be the most exciting reward in agility training, get your dog used to this unique obstacle by first calling him through, as you did with the open tunnel.

1. If you can remove the cloth section from the barrel section of this obstacle, that is a good way to start. Otherwise, begin with Step 2. Follow exactly the same steps that you did for the open tunnel. First, call your dog through the barrel. Run with your dog as he runs through, and finally, send your dog.

Then attach the cloth section onto the barrel and continue with the following.

Teaching the closed tunnel takes more time than the open tunnel, because the dog must learn to push through a dark chute.

Training for Agility

2. Roll the chute material as if you are rolling a shirtsleeve to make it as short as possible. With a friend holding your dog at the entry, hold the material wide open and call your dog. Repeat many times until your dog runs through enthusiastically.

3. Gradually unroll the chute, but hold it open and call your dog through. Continue until the chute is its full length.

4. After many repetitions, begin dropping the cloth on your dog's back as he exits. Make sure it does not cover his head.

5. In small increments, drop the cloth earlier and earlier. The first few times the cloth covers his head, he should be inches (centimeters) from the end.

6. Continue to drop the cloth more quickly until your dog pushes through. Remember that once the dog is pushing through, you can use your voice to encourage him and to let him know where you will be when he exits.

Phase Two: Run With

As before, the purpose of this phase is to transition to moving together as a team. You will send your dog into the closed tunnel and then run to meet him at the end. It takes dogs a bit longer to perform this obstacle than the open tunnel, so you will need a bit more time to get there.

1. Have a friend hold the tunnel open, and put food on a target or drop a favorite toy so that your dog sees it.

1. Hold him by the collar.

2. Release him and, with the hand closest to him, use your bowling motion to indicate the tunnel.

3. If he runs around the tunnel, your partner should pick up the target or toy before the dog gets it.

4. If he runs through, he gets to eat the treat on the target or grab his toy.

5. Run along the tunnel and meet your dog at the far end as quickly as possible. Reinforce his behavior with extra treats or a game of tug.

6. Gradually have your partner drop the cloth on the dog as you did in the recall phase.

Phase Three: Send On

Even if you have fallen behind your dog on course, you want him to race into the closed

Teaching the Tunnels

tunnel and push through if it is the next obstacle. With this exercise, you hold back a bit while your dog moves ahead of you.

1. Have a friend hold the tunnel open a couple of times to get your dog warmed up. Then, assuming your dog is comfortable with pushing through, leave it closed.

2. Send your dog into the tunnel using your command and arm motion.

3. Unlike the first two exercises, don't rush forward this time. Hang back a bit more each time until you can stand near the entry while he completes the obstacle.

4. Throw your dog's toy, food bag, or a big treat so he sees it as he emerges. Once again, your timing is really important here. He should see the reward immediately and charge forward to get it.

5. After a few moments, run out and play with your dog, or open the food bag and deliver a treat where the bag landed.

Challenging Tunnel Entries

At the novice level, the entry to the tunnel is generally obvious to dogs. The only challenge may be getting the dog to enter at the correct end, as indicated by the judge. At more advanced levels, however, the tunnel entry may not be visible to the dog. It is important to teach dogs to seek out and take tunnel entries that they may not be able to see. The next page features examples of simple and difficult tunnel entries.

Above left, from top:
First, roll the chute and call your dog through.
Reinforce your dog for running through.
Run with and then send on your dog.
Gradually drop the cloth on your dog until he has to push through.

Training for Agility

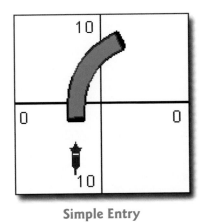

Simple Entry

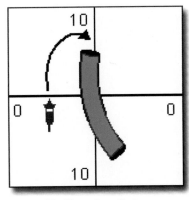

Challenging Entry

A simple exercise can train a dog who thinks, "Okay. She said there was a tunnel out here somewhere." Start by letting your dog see the tunnel entry, and send him through. Give him his usual reinforcement in the form of a treat on a target or a toy that you placed on the ground beyond the tunnel exit. Then, very gradually, in small increments, work your way back from the entry so that it becomes less and less visible. Send your dog from each new location. The pattern will look like the example below, right:

Then, do a mirror image of the exercise by curving the tunnel in the other direction and switching sides so that the dog must turn left into the tunnel. Rather than putting your reward on the ground, as you have been doing, send your dog into the tunnel, then toss the toy or a food-stuffed bag ahead of your dog just as he exits the tunnel. This is a powerful strategy, because it taps into his inherent prey drive. Tossing a reward is good for all dogs, but it is particularly useful with a dog who becomes savvy and runs around the tunnel to get the food on the target, or if the dog goes through the tunnel too slowly.

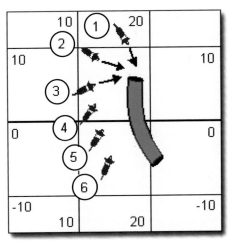

Tunnel Entry Exercise

Teaching the Tunnels

Chapter Eleven

Teaching the A-Frame and Dogwalk

Section I

The contact obstacles—the A-frame, teeter, and dogwalk—present unique agility challenges. These three obstacles are called *contacts*, because each has a zone the dog must touch with one or more feet to receive "credit" for performing the obstacle. It is particularly satisfying to teach your dog to fly up and over the A-frame and to race full tilt across the dogwalk, stopping smartly in the contact zone. (We'll look at the teeter in a separate chapter, because this obstacle, with its amusement-park-ride motion, has its own unique training challenges.)

Contact zones, on both the ascending and descending sides of these obstacles, were created to keep dogs from leaping on or off the equipment in an unsafe manner. Some organizations require that the dog touch both the up and down zones. Other organizations require that the dog enter the zone on the downside only. In reality, few dogs, other than those with giant strides, have trouble touching the upside contact; however, the downside contact is a challenge for every agility dog in one way or another. Left to their own devices, big dogs and medium dogs love to sail over this area. Even small dogs, if given the chance, will launch off the A-frame or dogwalk above the contact zone in a poor imitation of the Wright brothers. To help dogs recognize the contact zone, this section is always painted a different color from the obstacle—generally yellow, which is visible to dogs.

All agility organizations take the contact zones very seriously. A dog judged to have missed touching the zone during a competitive trial receives either a stiff point penalty or is automatically disqualified for that run. Beyond the novice level, all missed contacts are a disqualification. The bottom line? Teach your dog to perform the contact zone correctly from the beginning.

Two-Part Training

There are two distinct parts to teaching the contact obstacles:

- teaching the dog to complete the obstacle itself
- teaching the dog to perform the contact zone

In Section I of this chapter, we'll look at teaching your dog to complete the A-frame and dogwalk obstacles. These two contact obstacles are similar in that dogs must run up an incline and run down the opposite side. The A-frame adds the variable of steepness that the dog must learn to negotiate at good speed. The challenge of the dogwalk is the narrowness of the plank.

In Section II of this chapter, we'll look at teaching your dog to successfully negotiate the contact zones on the A-frame and dogwalk.

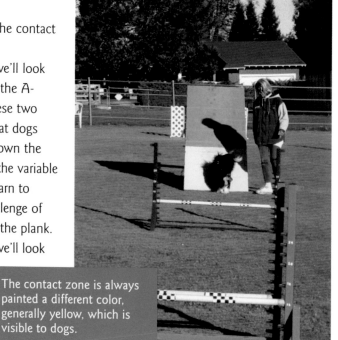

The contact zone is always painted a different color, generally yellow, which is visible to dogs.

Training for Agility

Agility Speak

Discussions about contacts can be a bit confusing, because agility competitors use the term in two different ways. First, the word *contacts* is used to refer to the three contact obstacles (A-frame, teeter, and dogwalk) themselves. For example, one might say, "In Jumpers classes, there are no contacts," which means, of course, that Jumpers courses have no contact obstacles. Alternately, the term is used to refer to the special area that the dog must touch close to the base of each contact obstacle. One frequently hears handlers say, "My dog blew her contact," meaning that she performed the obstacle but failed to touch the contact zone. In cases where I think you might be confused, I will use the terms *contact obstacle* or *contact zone*.

The Mark of Success

To be accomplished on the A-frame, the dog must:

- Generate adequate speed to climb without struggling
- Place one or more feet in the upside contact zone
- Show no hesitation at the apex and even "catch some air" by jumping over the peak
- Descend under control but without losing speed
- Place one or more feet in the downside contact zone

    Similarly, efficient and safe dogwalk performance requires the dog to:

- Get all four feet on the obstacle and keep them on all the way across
- Place one or more feet in the upside contact zone
- Maintain speed across the flat portion of the dogwalk
- Descend under control but without losing speed
- Place one or more feet in the downside contact zone

Obstacle Commands

The most common commands for the A-frame are *climb* or *scramble*. The terms selected most often for the dogwalk are *walk it*, *walk up*, *plank*, and *bridge*.

Teaching the A-Frame

The typical method for teaching this obstacle is quite simple:

Purchasing the A-Frame and Dogwalk

These two obstacles represent a considerable monetary investment. If you decide to buy one or both, be sure that they have a stable, metal base for your dog's safety. The surfaces that the dog will run on should be well painted and coated with a nonskid surface. There should be cross slats to provide purchase for the dog. The best obstacles are all aluminum rather than part plywood. (This is great if you need to keep the obstacle outside, because the plywood will eventually warp.) The A-frame must be adjustable, so that you can set it at different training heights. The ideal dogwalk is also adjustable, but it is more difficult to find.

If your backyard will not accommodate a dogwalk or A-frame, you can make a small training device that simulates a dogwalk on one side and an A-frame on the other. It is particularly useful for teaching the two-on/two-off contact, and it makes an excellent transition between stair contacts and full-sized equipment contacts. Plans for building a contact trainer are included in Appendix I. (This device is also helpful for working a running contact with small dogs and medium dogs.)

1. Lower the A-frame so that the peak is only 3 (0.9 m) or 4 feet (1.2 m) high.
2. Put your dog on a fairly short lead, and hold it with the hand closest to the obstacle. Load treats into your other hand.
3. Approach the A-frame, and with your voice, encourage your dog to climb. If he balks at all, lure him with a piece of food.
4. When he reaches the top, don't allow him to pause.
5. Using your voice and a lure, if needed, encourage him to descend.

In training the A-frame, the dog should be kept on lead until he is very comfortable with performing the obstacle and there is no danger that he will run around it. Try to manage your dog so that the leash does not tighten, however. That can slow him down, and you never want to communicate to your dog that agility is a leisurely game.

When your dog is comfortable with the A-frame, the obstacle should be raised incrementally until he can perform it at full height.

Teaching the A-Frame for Speed

The traditional style of teaching the A-frame, that which I just described, sometimes

Accomplished dogs race up and over the A-frame.

results in a dog who descends slowly. A second way to teach this obstacle is favored by people who want to be highly competitive. It is called *back-chaining*. The focus is on teaching the dog to run fast downhill before tackling the obstacle as a whole.

To back-chain the A-frame, follow these steps:

1. Put your dog on a short leash so that you can control his movement.
2. Lift your dog, or for big dogs, lure your dog onto the downside of the A-frame and then turn him to face toward the bottom. His first position should be just a few feet (meters) from the base.
3. Have your partner place your target, a plastic lid with a piece of food on it, off the end of the obstacle, leaving room for your dog's front feet to hit the ground and his back feet to stay on the obstacle.
4. In an excited voice, encourage your dog to run down to the target. Repeat the exercise from the same height until he is confident running down at the speed you want. Gradually lift or lure him to a higher position on the A-frame, and work that height until you are pleased with the speed. Keep increasing the height of your dog's position in small increments until he will run down full speed from the apex to the bottom.

A-Frame Heights

Most agility organizations set the apex of the A-frame at 5 feet 6 inches (167.6 cm). In USDAA, bigger dogs—those who measure more than 16 inches (40.6 cm) at the withers—climb an A-frame set at 6 feet 3 inches (190.5 cm).

Teaching the A-Frame and Dogwalk

5. Introduce him to the whole obstacle as described above (the main method of teaching the A-frame).

6. In increments, raise the A-frame to its full height. If your dog slows down as the downside gets steeper, repeat the back-chaining process again until he regains confidence. Then, try the whole obstacle again.

Teaching the Dogwalk

The dogwalk is a bit more challenging for dogs, particularly larger breeds. The dogwalk is 12 inches (30.5 cm) wide, so it requires a dog to control the placement of all four feet while moving quickly.

This obstacle also presents more danger: Dogs can fall if a foot goes over the edge. A dog who slips can be hurt or scared and take months to retrain. Thus, it is wise to make sure your dog understands the idea of staying on a narrow board. I hope that you have played the coordination games in Chapter 6; here is another good warm-up game for the dogwalk.

The dogwalk requires a dog to control the placement of all four feet while moving quickly.

Training for Agility

Walking the Plank

1. Find a wooden plank about 12 inches (30.5 cm) wide. Place it flat on the ground. Help your dog onto the plank with a lure. You may need to keep him on a fairly short leash initially. Guide him to walk, trot, or run on the plank to the end. Give a treat at the end. If a foot slips off the board, don't correct in any way. Just help him back on and reinforce the behavior when he stays on.

2. After completing one direction, make sure your dog comes straight off the end of the board rather than the side of the board. You want to make sure that he understands how to get on and off in a straight line.

3. When your dog understands the game, remove the leash. Over several days, work with your dog to encourage him to race back and forth on the board. Race, of course, is a relative term with the giant breeds, but encourage as much speed as your dog can handle. Make the game fun using your tone of voice and use of treats.

4. When your dog is very comfortable with the game, raise one end of the plank a few inches (centimeters). It can be elevated on bricks or blocks of wood as long as the plank is stable. For small dogs, the side of an agility table is a nice height. Now, ask your dog to race up and down the board. You should provide positive reinforcement at each end.

When this exercise is a piece of cake, elevate both ends of the board to the height of a concrete block. Your dog will need to jump on the end. Again, work to get him to move briskly back and forth. Continue to make this an exciting game. When he is comfortable with the plank, he is more than ready to tackle the dogwalk itself.

The Baby Dogwalk

It is ideal to start your dog on a training dogwalk that is much closer to the ground than the competition obstacles. For their novice classes, most teachers have a dogwalk that is only 2 (0.6 m) or 3 feet (0.9 m) off the ground.

Teaching the dogwalk is very similar to teaching the A-frame:

1. Have your dog on a fairly short lead, and hold treats in your other hand (the one farthest from the dog). Approach the dogwalk and encourage your dog to get on. If he hesitates, lure him with a piece of food.

2. If your dog is hesitant or anxious, drop treats at intervals across the obstacle. Your

dog can graze all the way across for a few repetitions. Space the food out farther and farther as the dog becomes relaxed, then fade it out.

Because of the safety factor, two things are very important in handling the dogwalk. First, you should remain even with your dog's head. If you get ahead, he may be tempted to jump. Second, make sure to have your teacher or a friend walk on the far side directly across from you to prevent your dog from bailing off the side of the obstacle or flipping off at the end.

Stick with the baby dogwalk until your dog is very comfortable and can travel across briskly with no hesitation. It is ideal if your dog runs, but some large breeds simply have to trot. Again, watch your leash management so that you don't slow your dog down inadvertently.

The Full-Size Dogwalk

No surprises here. Just repeat what you did to teach the baby obstacle. Should your dog ever slip, don't make a big fuss about it. Scout the Sheltie never missed a step in training, but in her first year of trialing, she slipped on the dogwalk just as she reached the horizontal plank and flew off like a platform diver. She landed on her feet but looked startled. Fortunately, I just laughed. She shook herself, and we took off for the next obstacle, since most trial rules don't allow you to redo a contact obstacle. Fortunately, she never showed the least hesitation at the dogwalk during her subsequent runs.

I know what you are thinking: If I want to be highly competitive, should I back-chain the dogwalk like I did the A-frame? You absolutely can do this with small- and medium-sized dogs, but it is very difficult to lure big dogs on the dogwalk and get them to turn around on such a narrow plank.

Now, let's take a look at your options for handling the contact zones when your dog reaches the bottom of the A-frame and dogwalk.

Section II

Teaching your dog to run across the A-frame and dogwalk is only the first half of teaching these obstacles. Next, he must learn to perform the contact zones found at both ends of the contact obstacles. In competition, a dog receives credit for "making his contact" if he gets a minimum of one foot (or part of one foot) in the contact zone. A dog can be immensely talented in agility, but if he does not understand how to consistently touch the contact zones, he will have limited success in competition.

Training for Agility

Dogs must be taught to consistently touch the contact zone.

While contact zones are present on both the up and downsides of the contact obstacles, most dogs, other than those with huge strides, experience no difficulty with the upside. The downside contact, on the other hand, is the bane of many agility dogs.

The Upside Contact Zone

For the majority of dogs, you have no need to worry about teaching a touch in the upside contact. They simply run through the zone since they are going uphill. However, a few dogs who are extremely powerful and have huge strides can leap halfway up the obstacle. I recently had a Standard Poodle in class who didn't even come close to the contact zone once he was really running. For these athletes, you must teach them to run through the upside contact zone.

Two techniques will encourage a solid performance:

I. Construct an arch that is just tall enough for your dog to run underneath. For example, many people cut a hula hoop in half. Others piece together pieces of PVC. Whatever you use, create a system to stick the arch in the ground so that it straddles the upside of the contact obstacle. The goal is that the dog must run under the arch to get on the

Teaching the A-Frame and Dogwalk

contact. Because he can't lift his head high, he will be unable to leap at the obstacle. Practice with the arch regularly until your dog learns the routine of running up. When he appears to understand the idea, alternate your practice sessions with it on and off. Bring the arch out any time you see the old leaping behavior rear its head.

2. Put something desirable to the dog on the upside of the contact. This can be a high-value treat or even a treat on a target. Whichever you use, place it against a slat so that it doesn't roll down. (The position will vary based on the size of your dog.) The goal is to get the target set so that the dog must run up to get it, and he won't get it if he leaps. If you are using your target, you can click the touch and deliver a second treat. The challenge here is that the dog must now climb the remainder of the A-frame from a standstill. If this strains your dog, don't use this method. However, most dogs strong enough to leap the contact do not find this to be a problem.

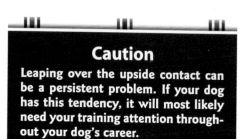

Caution

Leaping over the upside contact can be a persistent problem. If your dog has this tendency, it will most likely need your training attention through-out your dog's career.

Downside Contact Zones

Dogs can get this part of the job done in two ways. Many dogs are taught to stop at the bottom of the contact with their front feet on the ground and their hind feet on the obstacle. This type of performance is called *two on/ two off.* Although the two-on/ two-off method guarantees that the dog will touch the contact zone, it takes a bit more time, because the dog hesitates in the contact zone, at least briefly.

The second approach to handling this part of the obstacle is called a *running contact.* That is, the dog is taught to run right to the bottom and off the A-frame or dogwalk without stopping. The running contact is obviously the fastest, but it sometimes leads to dogs launching off the obstacle without touching the contact zone. On the other hand, the running contact is easier on some breeds' shoulders and backs because it doesn't require the dog to slam to a stop.

If you are training your first dog, I strongly recommend the two-on/two-off approach unless you have specific health concerns about him. This method, if well taught and regularly reinforced, is much more likely to give your dog solid contacts. In addition, it allows you to catch up with your dog—an important consideration given that the dog often needs to turn to another obstacle upon completion of the dogwalk or A-frame. If your dog has blasted off the end of the obstacle before you even arrive, it puts you in a very bad position to stay on course.

Although I taught Scout the Sheltie a lovely two-on/two-off contact that has been my best training investment, with Grace the Corgi I opted for a running contact on the A-frame to save her back. It means that our runs have an out-of-control quality since no pause occurs on that contact obstacle where we can check in with each other. I also have a concern that over the course of her agility career, she may start leaping off the A-frame above the contact zone.

The downside contact is the most challenging for the majority of dogs.

The Mark of Success

To get "credit" for performing the contact, only one dog toe must touch inside the zone. As you can imagine, such a close call is not desirable. If the judge is out of position, it is very easy to miss seeing incidental contact. To be proficient at performing the contact zones, your dog should clearly get all four feet into the contact zone, and then, if doing a two-on/two-off contact, stop in that position and stay until released, or if doing a running contact, run right to the very bottom of the obstacle and off without hesitating.

Obstacle Commands

Handlers who teach the two-on/two-off contact generally use the *touch* or *target* command. The command should be given as soon as the dog starts downhill on the A-frame or dogwalk. For dogs taught a running contact, handlers generally give no command.

The two-on/two-off method is most likely to give your dog solid contacts.

Teaching Two-On/Two-Off

Traditionally, this style of contact has been taught at the same time as the dog is learning the contact obstacle itself. More recently, trainers have begun teaching the two on/two off before the dog even gets on the equipment. Let's take a look at both methods.

On the Equipment Your dog should have learned the *touch* command thoroughly. (See Chapter 4.) This means that your dog will consistently touch a target, such as a plastic lid, with his nose or feet when asked. By using this command, you will be able to stop your dog in the correct position on the contact obstacle.

Before you put a dog on the equipment, place your target on the grass at a distance from the obstacle that will allow your dog to stop comfortably with his front feet on the ground and back feet on the obstacle. For Scout the Sheltie, this is about 6 inches (15.2 cm) from the end of the obstacle. For a high-drive Lab, the target will be more than 1 foot (0.3 m) off the end of the obstacle. For small dogs, this may be a few inches (centimeters). For big dogs, the space will be considerably longer. Experiment with your dog to find the right distance.

Now you are ready to go. As discussed earlier, you are going to lure or encourage your dog up the A-frame or across the dogwalk. Your training partner should be on the opposite side to prevent your dog from slipping or jumping off. Both of you should move quickly to stay even with your dog's head. When he starts down the ramp:

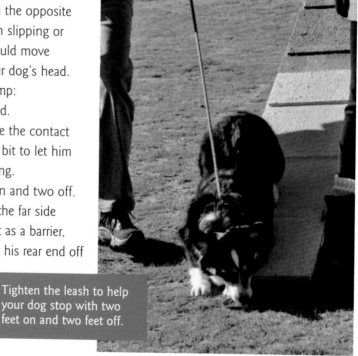

1. Give your *touch* command.
2. A few feet (meters) before the contact zone, tighten the leash a bit to let him know that a stop is coming.
3. Stop him with two feet on and two off.
4. Your friend's position on the far side of the obstacle should act as a barrier, keeping him from flipping his rear end off the obstacle. If he starts to flip off on your side, your legs should block him.

Tighten the leash to help your dog stop with two feet on and two feet off.

Training for Agility

5. When he touches the lid, click and reinforce with a toy or treat.

If he doesn't touch the lid, put a treat on the target a few times so that he sees it. As he reaches for the treat, click and offer a second treat. If he doesn't appear to recognize the *touch* command you already taught him, return to more *touch* practice away from the equipment.

Repeat this activity many times with your dog on lead. Remember that your goal is to train a dog who runs right to the end of the obstacle and then plants himself with two feet on and two off. You don't want to train your dog to creep down into the contact zone. Try to manage your leash so that your dog can travel as quickly as he wants but can't shoot off the end of the obstacle. Yes, this is an art.

Your dog should stay on the contact zone until released. This means you must use the release word you taught him during obedience training. Use the word *okay* or any other comfortable word. If you just take off running without a formal release, your dog will take charge of deciding when he is ready to go on. In summary, your series of commands for the dogwalk would sound like, "walk it, touch, okay."

When your dog is performing the obstacle confidently, give your training partner a rest, and run your dog alone. If he starts flipping his rear end off at the bottom of the contact zone, you might put up a small barrier such as a jump wing, as a reminder that he should keep his hind end on the obstacle.

Fade the use of the target when your dog understands his job performing the two-on/two-off contact. When you remove the target, give the *touch*

Your dog should stay on the contact until released.

Teaching the A-Frame and Dogwalk

Caution

A stunning number of agility competitors have no idea what their dog will do when they get to a contact obstacle in a trial. They whisper a prayer, they turn in three circles before going in the ring (it worked last weekend!), and they plead with the dog as he races toward the yellow contact zone: "Touch, touch, TOUCH." Since the dog has no real idea what his job is, the results are completely unpredictable. One time he gets a foot in the yellow, the next time he leaps over it entirely.

Take your time and teach a solid contact performance. This will require a sequential system such as I describe in this chapter that will train your dog to plant his feet exactly as you want at every contact. He will do this because he understands that his job is to do so and because he gets rewarded regularly for it.

command as you have been doing. When he bobs his head toward the target location, click and reinforce as if the target were there. You may put the target back periodically if your dog needs a reminder to stop and touch.

After weeks or months of repetition, when your dog is able to perform the obstacle and nail the contact without any restraint from the leash, remove it and let him try performing the obstacle loose, with you running close by. If he backslides and forgets to stop, put the leash back on. Even when he is getting a good grasp of stopping, I find it useful to go back and forth between leash work and running loose. Scout the Sheltie is a perfect illustration. As an adolescent, she was so excited in class that she always forgot to stop for her first contact. I didn't want to reinforce this behavior, so I kept her on leash for her initial A-frame or dogwalk, made sure she nailed the contact, and reinforced her profusely. After that, she calmed down and did them perfectly. It's up to you as the handler to find creative ways to ensure consistent good performances from your dog.

Without Equipment Although many good dogs have been trained to do the contact obstacles as described, a new training trend makes a lot of sense, even for people who have unlimited access to equipment. Using this method, the dog is taught the two-on/two-off position as a separate skill before he ever tries the "real" contact obstacles. This process allows the dog to understand the expectation thoroughly before trying it during the intense excitement of performing the contact obstacles. Long term, it creates a more reliable contact, since your dog will have generalized the concept to a variety of locations.

This method employs steps or anything around your house that is wide enough for your dog to stand on that allows him to elevate his rear end a bit above his front end. One wide step is better than a flight of steps. For example, the wide one-step landing at my front door is a perfect training place. A flight of stairs can be used if that is what you have. Your goal in this work is to teach your dog to put his front feet on the ground, leave his hind end on the step, and touch a target on the ground. This simulates the position you want your dog to hold on the contacts. Here is how to proceed with the training:

You can teach two on/two off without agility equipment.

1. Using a treat, lure your dog to go all the way up on the step. Turn him around to face you with your lure.
2. Encourage him to step forward, but stop him with his back feet on the step and his front feet on the stoop below.
3. As soon as the dog is in that position, mark the behavior with your voice or clicker, and reinforce with a treat.
4. Use your formal release word to let your dog step down off the stair.
5. Repeat many times until your dog offers the two-on/two-off behavior any time you initiate the stair game.
6. Add your target in a spot that your dog will be able to touch when performing the two on/two off from the stair. Now, when you ask for the two-on/two-off behavior, use your touch command. Click and reinforce when your dog touches the target while keeping his hind end on the stair.

Teaching the A-Frame and Dogwalk

Agility Speak

Whether you are training the contact performance with or without equipment, the _touch_ command will come to mean "stop with two on/two off and touch the target." No separate command is used for the two-on/two-off position.

Initially, you may need to rotate in front of your dog as he assumes the two-on/two-off position to block him from continuing to walk forward. As he becomes comfortable, gradually move to his side until he performs correctly with you standing on either side, approximating your relative position on an agility course.

Be creative about locating places to practice this exercise. For example, another excellent area is the fireplace hearth. Lure your dog onto the hearth, turn him around, and then stop him with his two back feet on the hearth and two front feet off. If your house does not have stairs or a hearth, it is easy to construct a low platform that you can set up inside your home or out in your yard just by elevating a piece of plywood a few inches (centimeters) on one side.

As your dog begins to understand the concept, make it more challenging. Reward him for staying in place while you move in front of him. This is very important, because later you want to be able to switch sides while your dog holds the contact zone.

Once your dog is comfortable with the correct position, begin to "proof" him on holding his contacts. For example, tease him briefly with his toy and praise him if he restrains himself and holds his position. Once given the verbal release, reward him with a game of tug.

The experience of working on a variety of "obstacles" around your home will enable your dog to easily transfer these skills to the dogwalk and A-frame in class. Imagine how easy the whole contact obstacle will be when your dog just runs to the end, stops in the correct position on your command, and touches the target with his nose.

**Putting It All Together** When your dog is reliable in doing the two-on/two-off contact in a variety of places around the house, it's time to teach him to do the obstacle itself. Teach the dog to run across the A-frame or dogwalk, as described in Section I of this chapter. Remember to keep him on leash initially, using your training partner on the far side. As he approaches the contact zone, give your _touch_ command to tell him that you want him to stop with two on/two off at the bottom and touch the target. If he does, mark the behavior with your click or marker word, and jackpot the behavior with several cookies. Then, make sure to use your release word to let him get off.

Training for Agility

While your dog is new to this experience, reward each time that he crosses the obstacle and stops in position; however, when he understands what you want, you need to reinforce randomly. Trainers debate the frequency of reinforcement. I have found that giving a treat or playing with my experienced dogs approximately 50 percent of the time keeps them sharp and trying to do their best. You can, of course, use verbal praise every time your dog gets it right, even if you don't deliver a reward. When you plan to treat, you can click. On the repetitions where you just plan to praise, make sure not to click. When Scout the Sheltie nails her contact but I am not planning to treat, I just say, "You are the best!" It is also a great idea to pet your dog on occasion while he holds the contact.

What if the dog doesn't stop or flips around off the end? Remember, corrections have no place in agility. Just ignore the behavior, run the dog around to the other end or side of the contact obstacle, and run it again. Do what you need to do to create success, such as tightening your leash a bit or having your partner help block the dog from the side. When he does get it right, even with help, throw a party!

Teaching The Running Contact

There is considerable debate in the agility community about the running contact. Many trainers believe that a dog's stride determines his ability to perform the running contact. If a dog does not have space to take a last stride into the contact zone, he can either crash or jump off the obstacle. If you decide on a running contact, watch your dog closely during your early training to make sure that he is physically able to stride right to the bottom.

Two groups of trainers teach a running contact: those who want to make the international agility team and need to shave off hundredths of seconds and those who have dogs who might hurt themselves by stopping suddenly. The latter includes long-backed dogs

The running contact suits dogs who are small and who have long backs.

Caution

Resist the urge to begin competing until your dog can perform the
contact obstacles safely. Once dogs
learn to leap a contact zone in a
trial, it is very difficult to retrain
the correct performance.

like Dachshunds or Basset Hounds and some toy breeds.

Many top handlers with high-drive herding dogs give their dogs the *lie down* command on the contact obstacles. They don't actually want the dog to lie down, but they do want the dog to drop partway into a down while continuing to run. The idea is to slow the dog just enough to get him into the contact zone without losing too much forward momentum. If you have a dog who might fall into this category, find a good teacher who understands Border Collies and similar dogs.

When teaching the running contact, encourage your dog to run right to the very bottom and off the obstacle. You can teach this in the following way:

1. Drag your hand with the treat straight to the bottom of the contact zone and along the ground.

2. Deliver the treat from your hand when the dog has cleared the obstacle.

If your dog shows any indication that he would like to jump off before the contact zone, try these two easy strategies:

1. Put a target with food on it on the ground a few feet (meters) beyond the contact. The distance will vary by breed. In this case, the dog should just be able to get all four feet on the ground comfortably. This makes most dogs run to the bottom and then off, rather than jumping, because they don't want to risk leaping over the treat.

2. Put a jump set at 4 inches (10.2 cm) quite close to the base of the contact. For a toy breed, this

Some big dogs also do a running contact, which shaves off time.

Training for Agility

Alternative Strategies for Teaching the Running Contact

Two other strategies are helpful to teaching a running contact. One idea is to place a low jump just 1 foot (0.3 m) or so from the base of the contact obstacle. If the dog runs to the bottom, he will have no problem taking the jump. If the dog launches, he will land on the jump, and that is not comfortable. Most dogs seem to recognize this scenario and choose to run down. This behavior builds the muscle memory of the running contact. Some trainers construct a PVC arch just tall enough for their dog to run under at the bottom of the contact. This forces the dog to keep his head down and prevents a jump.

will be just 1 (0.3 m) or 2 feet (0.6 m) away. For a big breed, it may be 4 (1.2 m) or 5 feet (1.5 m). Again, the correct distance is when your dog can just get all four feet on the ground before he needs to jump. Since the dog sees the jump on the descent and does not want to crash the jump, he will run to the bottom and then take the jump.

For both these methods, when your dog seems patterned on running to the bottom, alternate having the target or the jump in place and then gone. Gradually fade these "props." If your dog consistently returns to leaping off the contact high in the contact zone, I strongly recommend that you switch methods and teach the two-on/two-off. Otherwise, you will spend your dog's entire career hoping that he touches the contact on virtually every run.

Do not be misled into believing that, as I once did, small dogs will stay on the entire contact obstacle. Tucker the Papillon is a poster child for the reality that toy breeds are very capable of missing the contacts. When he is running down the A-frame or dogwalk and sees a tunnel straight ahead, he can clear the contact zone without even trying.

The Work Never Ends

It is very common for dogs to have terrific contacts in practice and then levitate over the contact zone in a trial. Whenever they are in the same room, agility trainers debate the best training methods and retraining methods for contacts. Just keep in mind that whatever method you choose, you and your dog will most likely work on his contacts throughout his agility career.

Chapter Twelve

Teaching the Teeter

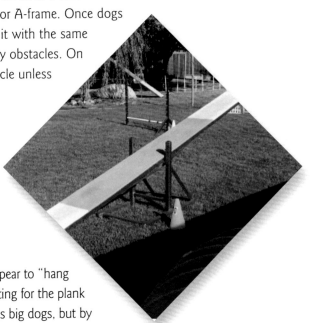

The teeter is the third contact obstacle, which I promised to deal with separately. Because the teeter moves, it involves a different approach to training than does the dogwalk or A-frame. Once dogs understand the teeter, though, they perform it with the same confidence and exuberance as they do the stationary obstacles. On the flip side, dogs can get spooked about this obstacle unless training is slow and methodical.

Mark of Success

To perform the teeter well, the dog must:

- Race up the teeter with no hesitation
- Understand the pivot point and stop there or even closer to the end to shift the balance
- Wait until the plank hits the ground
- Run off through the contact zone

Like hot-shot surfers, the best-performing dogs appear to "hang ten" as they stand poised at the end of the teeter, waiting for the plank to hit the ground. Toy dogs can do the teeter as well as big dogs, but by necessity, they must run way out on the plank for the balance to shift.

Purchasing a Teeter

Purchasing a teeter is a moderate monetary investment in the range of agility obstacles. The teeter consists of two parts, a base and the plank. The base should be a sturdy, stable metal tripod that allows the plank to be set at at least three training heights. The plank may be wood, although those made of aluminum have a much longer life. Either way, the plank should be painted and coated with a nonskid surface.

Obstacle Commands

The most common command for this obstacle is simply the word *teeter*. Other commands are *seesaw*, *tip*, and *tip it*. Some handlers say, "Easy teeter" to help the dog recognize that he needs to slow down a bit.

Preparing for the Teeter

Remember the game called *Walking the Plank* (see Chapter 11) that I suggested for getting your dog ready for the dogwalk? That game is also terrific for the teeter, because it teaches your dog to negotiate a narrow board. You can add a teeter-specific twist to the game. Once your dog is comfortable negotiating the plank on the ground, place a round object such as a pipe or length of PVC under the center of the board so that it tips back and forth. You might want to put your dog back on leash until he is comfortable with the minor movement. Remember to praise and reinforce him when he runs right to the end. When the activity is easy for your dog while on lead, repeat the activity with your dog off lead. As before, make sure that your dog always runs straight off the board when you release him.

Teaching the Teeter

Ideally, the process of teeter instruction is taught in two phases: first, the baby teeter, followed by the full-sized teeter. The baby teeter looks like the official obstacle except it drops only a few inches (centimeters). Even though the baby teeter does not drop very far,

Agility Speak

In competition, a dog is penalized for a *fly off* if he leaps off the teeter before the board hits the ground. This is one of the more subjective aspects of agility, so it is important to train your dog to hang on until there is no doubt in anyone's mind that the teeter is down.

Training for Agility

some agility teachers bungee a piece of foam or pillow on the underside to pad the landing and minimize any jarring sensation for the dog.

The Baby Teeter

The teeter is best taught initially by two people, according to the following steps:

1. Start by having your training partner crouch at the high end of the teeter to support the board.

2. With your dog on leash, encourage him onto the board and walk him toward the high end. Use a lure to keep him moving and to help him keep all four feet on the obstacle.

3. As he arrives at the high end, your partner should lower the board as slowly as possible to avoid surprising the dog. Obviously, this is easier with a Sheltie than a Newfoundland, but do whatever you can to ensure that the dog has a positive experience on the short ride down.

4. After many repetitions, let the board drop a bit, but have your partner catch it before it crashes down.

5. Gradually increase the distance until the board hits the ground on its own.

   Remember to practice this exercise on both sides of the teeter so that your dog is equally comfortable wherever you are. When your dog understands the game, try it off lead.

The Contact Zone

Like the A-frame and dogwalk, the teeter has a contact zone that the dog must

The baby teeter looks like the official obstacle except it drops only a few inches (centimeters).

Teaching the Teeter

Sound Sensitivity

Occasionally, a dog will be afraid of the noise that the teeter makes when it hits the ground. This is particularly common with herding breeds. If the teeter is lowered gently during training, the noise is dulled. If your dog does become nervous, desensitize him to the noise.

With your training partner at the teeter, take him far enough from the obstacle so that he is unconcerned when it is pushed to the ground. Then, while your partner bangs the teeter on the ground, feed or play with your dog. Repeat this process many times, gradually moving the dog closer to the teeter, by millimeters, without getting a fear response. When he will stand, eat, and play next to the banging teeter, he is ready to return to learning to ride the obstacle.

enter with at least one foot. There are three ways for him to do the teeter contact:

1. The traditional method is for the dog to pause at the teeter's pivot point, let the board drop, and then run off. This approach almost guarantees that the dog will "hit" the contact zone because he doesn't have enough momentum to leap over it. The problem is that it is very slow and gobbles up precious seconds. If you are someone who prefers a low-risk approach, you can teach this type of performance by stopping your dog at the pivot point during training on the baby teeter.

2. A second method is to run the dog into the contact zone and right to the end of the teeter. Once the dog reaches the edge, you have one of two choices. Many handlers, including me, let our dogs stand. All of them learn to crouch on their own to soften the landing. Other handlers ask their dogs to lie down, and the dogs ride to the ground in a *sphinx down*. If you have a dog with a good *down* and want to save stress on his shoulders and

The teeter has a contact zone that the dog must enter with at least one foot.

minimize the jarring as the teeter hits the ground, I suggest this option. In either case, this approach to performing the teeter lowers the teeter more quickly than stopping at the pivot point. To teach it, lure the dog to the end of the plank, and then give him treats from your hand as the board is lowered, or lure him into a *down* and give him treats as your partner lowers the board.

3. If you want to live on the edge and compete with the best, method three exists. It is the two-on/two-off method with which you are familiar from the previous chapter. It is the fastest and also riskiest strategy because it puts the dog in a position to bounce off when the teeter hits the ground. Once they grasp the concept, though, most dogs seem quite comfortable with the move.

   To teach this style, use your target. Position it the same distance off the teeter that you use for the dogwalk. Run your dog right to the end, watch carefully for the moment when the board is nearing the ground, and give your *touch* command. Clearly, this takes some fine timing and lots of practice. Running this far out lowers the teeter very quickly and leaves the dog in the perfect position for the next obstacle.

The Big Teeter

Once your dog can perform the baby teeter off lead with speed and nail his contact using whichever style you have chosen, you are ready to move him up to the full-sized obstacle.

Teeter Specifications

For agility trials, the high end of the teeter is between 24 inches (61.0 cm) and 27 inches (68.6 cm) from the ground. Each agility organization has additional requirements for this obstacle. For example, the AKC rules state that the teeter must be 12 inches (30.5 cm) wide, 12 feet (3.7 m) long, and must hit the ground in three seconds when a 3-pound (1.4 kg) weight is placed within 12 inches (30.5 cm) of the end.

1. Start with the big teeter at its lowest height, which is generally about half of competition height.
2. Put your dog back on lead and repeat the baby teeter training. Make sure you use your training buddy again to control the teeter's descent.
3. As with the baby teeter, gradually let the teeter drop in very small increments before letting your dog ride it all the way down.
4. As with the A-frame and dogwalk, always use your release word to let your dog move off the teeter. If the dog is allowed to release himself, you greatly raise the chance of a

Teaching the Teeter

fly off, because he will want to take off for the next obstacle rather than wait for you to give him the command when the teeter is safely on the ground.

Problem Solving the Teeter

Some dogs are suspicious of the teeter, despite your best training. You may need to get creative as a dog trainer.

I have found useful two strategies to be useful. For some dogs, it is helpful if they don't see the teeter move. You can remove the visual cues by stretching one agility tunnel along each side of the teeter. Because the teeter will be set just inches (centimeters) off the ground, having a tunnel on either side creates a corridor through which you can easily lure your dog. If this reassures your dog, practice in this way until your dog is relaxed even when you let the low teeter drop.

Many people with dogs who are anxious on the teeter have created a market for liverwurst and cheese from a can. Try making a "yellow brick road" along the teeter with dabs of the soft meat or cheese. You may need to purchase your own teeter to do this, since your

When you progress to the big teeter, put it on a low height.

Training for Agility

teacher may not want her teeter smelling like a smorgasbord. Again, make sure do to this with the teeter set very low and a friend holding and lowering the board initially.

Take Your Time

The teeter is much like an amusement park ride for your dog. If you take your time to progress through these steps—I am talking months here—he will get right back in line to do it again. If you speed up the process and let him get scared, he will dig in his heels, and you will need to start from scratch.

It is important to know that the teeter probably looks like the dogwalk to the inexperienced dog. When Tucker the Papillon was in one of his first fun matches, he raced up the teeter and right off the end at full bore. The crowd gasped as he did an imitation of Superman without the cape. Fortunately, he landed without getting hurt or scared. Such is not always the case.

When your dog is still inexperienced on the full-sized teeter, I suggest a safety precaution: When you arrive at class or at a fun match, take your dog to the teeter and have him perform the obstacle two or three times by itself. In a class setting, you might even practice the teeter on leash the first time, just to be sure you can stop

Caution

Sometimes even dogs who have been fine with the teeter become fearful. You cannot simply train through the fear. Start over from the beginning, with the teeter set at its lowest level, and make teeter training highly rewarding.

your dog. Once he recognizes the obstacle as the teeter, rather than the dogwalk, less chance exists that he will fly off when he encounters it during the lesson or run.

Teeter training should take months, but it is time well spent. I guarantee that you will feel a thrill when your dog races fearlessly up a full-height teeter, slams to a halt at the outer edge, and races off after the teeter hits the ground.

Teaching the Table

The table obstacle was originally included in agility to demonstrate that a dog cannot only run and jump, but he can also stop and wait. To perform the table, a dog must jump up onto the table and either sit or down for five seconds, depending on the position the judge has selected for that class. The judge counts the five seconds aloud. When the judge is finished counting and says, "Go!" the handler can call the dog off the table and resume the high-speed portion of the game.

The table is just that: a table between the size of an end table and a coffee table. The height of the table is adjusted for different-sized dogs, the same as the jumps. To raise and lower the table, legs of different lengths are attached. The surface is generally rough, to help the dogs stop without slipping off.

Although the table may sound straightforward, it is challenging for dogs who don't like to stop running. Scout the Sheltie, typical of many high-powered dogs, has failed to earn qualifying scores in dozens of trials as a result of doing something that resembles push-ups on the table, so that she can get back to the "real" game.

Purchasing a Table

The table is a useful obstacle to own because you can move it inside during the winter to continue to play table games. Keep in mind that constructing a table is right below the jumps in terms of simplicity. (See Appendix I for details.)

Construction of tables varies widely. The base may be PVC, wood, or metal, while the deck may be plywood or aluminum. In either case, the top should be painted and coated with a nonskid surface.

Whatever the material, the table should be sturdy for dogs of any size. In addition, the legs should be easy to change to the correct height for different-sized dogs. Last, the table should be light enough to move.

Some tables come with just one-size legs, and you may need to pay extra if you want other sets of legs. You will find a number of options for purchase by doing an Internet search for "agility tables."

The table is one of those obstacles that everyone should have at home. Regular practice of the games described later will help your dog enjoy the table as much as the other obstacles.

The Mark of Success

There are three distinct markers of an exemplary table performance. First, the dog should run directly to the table and get on. Second, the dog should lie down or sit immediately. Last, the dog should remain in that position for the full five seconds. For generations of agility dogs, these three behaviors were taught together. As a result, many dogs performed the table as if they were children being sent to their rooms, because the table interrupted all the excitement of running. Most trainers now teach each of these components separately so they are more fun and earn more rewards, and then chain them together.

To be accomplished on the table, your dog must:

- Run directly to the table without slowing down
- Get up on the "front" of the table (the side closest to the previous obstacle)
- Sit or down immediately without hesitation
- Show no interest in the judge, who may be standing quite close
- Remain in the *sit* or *down* until the judge finishes counting five seconds
- Wait to be released from the table

In addition, it is wise to train your dog to remain in the *sit* or *down* while you walk away from the table toward the next obstacle. This helps you to get a smooth start on the rest of the course.

Obstacle Commands

Handlers typically use the command *table* to direct the dog to this obstacle. Occasionally, a handler will select something different, such as *park it*.

Teaching the Table

The table training games described here can be done outside or inside as a great winter activity. A small modified table can be used for toy dogs. When not in use, the table should be put away or leaned against a wall so that it is special when you take it out. The moment the table comes out in my house, three dogs are on it, maneuvering for space, hoping for a treat. This is the attitude you are striving to create with this game.

To perform the table, a dog must jump up onto the table and either sit or down for five seconds.

Agility Speak

Before each class, the judge will provide a *briefing* for the competitors in that class. During the briefing for the Standard Class, the judge will tell the handlers whether she has selected a *sit* or a *down* on the table for that class.

Phase 1: Running to the Table and Getting On

1. Work with a partner initially. Have your partner stand behind the table with a treat on your target. Show your dog the food to get him excited, and then hold him back a few feet (meters) from the table. When he is focused on the table, let go. He will run onto the table to get the reward. If you use a clicker, click as soon as he gets all four feet on the table. If you are not clicker training, use a marker word such as "yes" to indicate to the dog that he has just done the right thing. In either case, reinforce the behavior with the treat. If your dog is nervous about getting on the table the first time, gently lift him on. It generally only takes one time to convince the dog that he won't get in trouble for "getting on the furniture." After rewarding your

dog, use your release word to let him get off the table. Repeat this exercise from all sides, and gradually lengthen the distance from which the dog runs to the table. Remember: Your dog should get up on the "front" of the table (the side away from your training partner); if he wants to duck around the back, have your partner lean across the table to lure him up on the correct side. In competition, getting up on the back side may result in a deduction of points.

Dogs should sit or down without an argument.

2. Working alone, put your target with food on the table. Holding his collar, walk your dog up to the table and show him the food, but don't let him have it. Get him excited with your voice: "Do you want that?" Walk him back a few feet (meters) from the table, still holding him. If he is focused on the table, let him go and run with him to the table. If he is eager to get on, stop in front of the table so that he stays on rather than jumping off the far side. If he is a bit reluctant, run past the table and turn to call him from the far side. When he gets on, click or mark the behavior. When he has eaten his treat, remember to use your release word so that he knows to get off the table. Repeat from all sides of the obstacle. When your dog is enthusiastically running to the table, gradually take him farther and farther back so that he learns to drive from a distance. If at any point in the process he races to the table and consistently slips or jumps off the far side, try saying his name just as he gets on the table. Generally, this will get him to put on the brakes and stay on the table. If he holds on, click and jackpot the success.

3. When your dog runs to the table happily, put the target on the table but without food on it. Hold your dog and get him revved up. Use your *table* command with a happy, musical voice as you let him go. Run with him to the table exactly as you have been doing. When he gets on the table, mark the correct behavior with your clicker or marker word, even if you are behind. It is desirable that your dog learns to drive ahead of you, but you should run quickly to meet him and immediately deliver the treat.

Training for Agility

4. Lastly, remove the target. Repeat all your previous steps, including running to the table, clicking, and delivering your treat. You should now have a dog who races to the table and leaps on enthusiastically.

Phase 2: Adding the *Down* or *Sit*

Your dog should be taught a fast *down* or *sit* away from the table. This is very important. Take a look at Chapter 5 if you need some details on obedience training for agility. If the dog is reluctant to perform these commands, it will get worse on the table. Move onto this second phase only when your dog is satisfactorily performing the down and *sit* away from the table.

At this stage, it is also very important that you think about body language. Many handlers unconsciously bend over their dogs to get them to down. Looming over a dog is read as intimidation by a canine. The dog may comply, but the dynamic creates a resistant, unhappy canine performer. Stand straight and neutral when you are near the table, and remember to keep your voice genuinely happy. It sometimes helps to turn slightly away from your dog and avert your eyes to avoid a power struggle. That said, here is how you should proceed:

1. Show your dog the table. He should get really excited and happy that the table game is beginning.
2. Send him to the table exactly as you have been practicing.
3. The second he is on the table, ask for a *sit* or *down*.
4. The moment his behind or belly hits the table, click, deliver a treat, and release. The treat should be given to the dog while he is sitting or lying down. The challenge is to make all of this happen extremely quickly. The

When asking your dog to down, turning away and averting your eyes may prevent a power struggle.

Teaching the Table

Caution

Be careful about asking your dog to sit stay or down stay on the table before he enjoys running to and jumping onto it to get rewards. If you do, your dog will associate the table with stopping the fun, and his table performance will become very slow, or he will even avoid the table.

sequence should flow like this: *table, sit* (or *down*), click (or "yes!"), treat, okay! Your timing is very important in this phase if your dog is to understand that speed pays off. Remember that you are reinforcing the speed of the *sit* and *down* only and not the whole table performance.

What if you ask for a *sit* or *down* and the dog doesn't respond or is terribly slow? Keep your voice neutral. You can say something like, "Uh oh," but without an edge. Just take the dog off the table by clapping or calling, and try it again with a happy voice. If the dog responds with the *sit* or *down*, click and respond immediately. If the dog doesn't respond again with the behavior you want, reteach the *sit* or *down* away from the table.

Phase 3: Extending the *Sit* and *Down* (for Five Seconds)

When your dog loves the game of running to the table, and his *sit* and *down* are done very fast, you can move onto this final phase. Randomly add very short *stays* after the dog sits or downs. While he is sitting or lying down, give him a series of treats to reinforce that you want him to stay. If he pops up from a *down* or lies down from a *sit* on his own, lure him back into his starting position, and then offer several treats while he holds it. When he has stayed as long as you want, praise and release him. Over time, vary your timing in your delivery of

Problem Solving

As with all the obstacles, unexpected things pop up, and you will have to think on your feet to find a training solution. For example, Grace the Corgi has such speed that she began flying off the far side of the table. Although she "knew" the table, I took a step back in the training process and put a target with a treat on the obstacle to remind her to stop. After a few repetitions, I removed the target. Then I tried the obstacle with her again, and when she dug in her nails to stop herself, I clicked and gave her a jackpot of treats. We repeated this several times before I asked her to sit or down, because I wanted her to know why she was getting a reward. Problem solved for now!

After your dog sits and downs quickly on the table, add short *stays*.

treats so that your dog never knows when his good behavior will result in a reward.

To keep the game fun, make sure that it is unpredictable. On some repetitions, for example, reward quick *sits* and *downs*. Then mix in *stays* of varying lengths. It is up to you whether you use the command *stay* or just assume that the *sit* and *down* implies that the dog should stay. Practice counting five seconds out loud to get your dog used to the sound. As he becomes confident with staying on the table, get a friend to act as a judge by standing close and counting for you.

Remember, the idea is to keep the table work fun, fast, and rewarding. The system described here works well with training young dogs, and it also can improve the performance of an experienced dog. You just might end up with a dog who thinks the table is the best obstacle on the course!

Teaching the Table

Chapter Fourteen

Teaching the Weave Poles

First, your dog dives into the correct entry—on the right side of the first pole. With his head down and eyes forward, he drives straight through the obstacle, barely bending around the poles, then races to the end and exits between the 11th and 12th poles.

To an agility trainer, nothing is as breathtaking as a speedy performance in the weave poles. In fact, it is a major accomplishment in dog training to teach your dog this behavior. There have been times in the ring when I have looked at my speedy Sheltie weaving her way through and exclaimed, "Wow, how did I teach her to do that?"

Novice classes generally have six poles. Beyond the beginning level, you generally encounter 12 poles, although judges occasionally throw in an unusual number such as 9.

Swift dogs can complete 12 weave poles in less than three seconds. Really. On the other hand, some dogs are painfully slow. In this chapter, I'll share training techniques that will develop your dog's confidence in doing the weave poles and maintain his drive to get through them as quickly as possible.

Purchasing Weave Poles

When you make the decision to purchase weave poles, you have a wider spectrum of choices than you do for other agility obstacles. Four types of poles are available. Let's take a look at all of the types, as well as their pros and cons:

1. **Set of 12 PVC poles with spikes on one end.** The spikes allow you to push them into the ground. Most have a strip of a flexible material that attaches the poles together so that it is easy to get the correct spacing.
   Advantage: Cost.
   Disadvantage: The dog does not get used to the metal-type base that he will encounter in trials. However, if you are just testing the agility waters, it is not a bad start.

2. **Set of poles made entirely from PVC.** The base is a long piece of PVC to which the poles themselves are attached. PVC legs extend to the side to create stability.
   Advantage: Cost.
   Disadvantages: First, these poles are not sturdy. If you have a high-drive dog who "attacks" the poles to get through, as he should, these will not hold up. More importantly, these poles require that the dog step back and forth across the PVC base. This does not encourage the dog to learn the correct footwork.

3. **Competition-type poles.** These poles have a flat, steel base with fixed poles. Cross support feet add stability and holes in those feet allow you to pin the obstacle to the ground using long spikes.
   Advantages: These poles last for generations of dogs, and they look exactly the same as the poles your dog will encounter when you trial.
   Disadvantages: They cost several times more than the first two options, and if you decide to use the channel method, you will need an entire second set of channel weaves.

4. **Metal base, competition-style poles.** These are the newest entry into the weave-pole market, and they can be adjusted to be used either as straight poles, or they can be staggered to create a channel. The poles are moved by sliding them off to the side on the stabilizer bars.
   Advantages: These types of poles provide the best of both worlds, and they should last a very long time.
   Disadvantage: Cost. However, they are cheaper than buying a set of channel weaves and a set of straight poles separately.

If you search for "agility weave poles" on the Internet, you will find plenty of possibilities.

Teaching this obstacle is likely to be the longest component of your agility training, because the weave poles don't resemble anything that a dog would choose to do on his own. It takes methodical and consistent work to help your dog understand what you want. It also requires a continuous effort to keep the weave poles fun over months of practice.

The Mark of Success

An outstanding performance at the weave poles requires that your dog:

- Find the weave pole entry from any angle
- Enter the weave poles between the first and second pole from the right side
- Weave in and out without skipping any poles and without being steered by the handler
- Keep his head down and look forward rather than at the handler
- Develop a technique for negotiating the poles quickly
- Exit on the left side if there is an even number of poles and on the right if there is an odd number

Obstacle Commands

Handlers generally use one of two commands: *weave* or *poles*. This obstacle is unique because many handlers chant the command while the dog is weaving, in the belief that verbal encouragement keeps the dog moving forward. I have found that Scout the Sheltie loves the weave song that sounds like, "Go poles, poles, poles, poles." Other dogs seem distracted by the noise. Try both approaches to see which works for your dog.

Novice classes generally have six poles.

Teaching the Weave Poles

Age Limitations

Dogs should not weave until they are at least one year old. Playing with tunnels and jumps with the bars laid on the ground is fine for puppies and young dogs, but weave poles are different. Weave poles require significant twisting, which is not healthy for a dog's developing skeletal structure. The dog may play in the channel weaves, but he should wait to bend around poles until his growth plates have closed.

Approaches to Teaching the Weave Poles

Theories about how to teach weave poles have expanded exponentially in recent years. In the end, there are still three popular methods.

Push-Pull

This is the traditional method of teaching the weave poles. The handler holds the dog on a short leash or tab and steers the dog by pushing him out between two poles and then pulling him back through the next space. The handler pushes and pulls until the dog makes it through all 6 or 12 poles. Many trainers encourage the dog to look forward by holding a toy or piece of food in front of him with the opposite hand and luring the dog in and out of the poles, in addition to steering with the leash. Needless to say, this method requires some serious coordination and the use of weave poles that are short enough to get your arm over the top.

This strategy has fallen out of favor with many trainers for two reasons. First, when they are steered with the leash, most dogs learn to weave through the poles in a pattern so excessively wide it eats up the seconds. It is much faster if a dog drives through the poles in as straight a line as possible. Second, few dogs learn to love the poles with this method because they do not enjoy being pushed and pulled. The result of this type of training is generally a slow, methodical dog.

Collar Weave

This method was initially developed by Border Collie handlers who assumed, correctly, that their Type A dogs would respond to a no-frills approach. Subsequently, this strategy has been successfully adopted by handlers with other medium- and large-size high-drive dogs. It is similar to the push-pull approach without all the fuss. Indeed, it is lovely in its simplicity. It requires no special equipment. The handler simply grasps the dog's collar and steers the dog through the weaves as fast as the dog will go. This method works best if you grasp the collar with your palm down, knuckles toward the front, and gently twist the collar at the correct moment to help your dog turn into the next pole. The handler strives to draw as straight a line as possible through the poles. If the dog has a lot of forward momentum and learns patterns easily, bingo—lightning weaves.

The collar weave method works well for high-drive dogs.

The downside is that this method doesn't work well with smaller, sensitive, or lower-drive dogs. Scout the Sheltie would have been horrified at being handled like this through the poles. Fortunately, another method called the *channel* method worked for her and will work for the majority of dogs.

Channel Method

In recent years, a new approach for teaching weaves has been wholeheartedly adopted by agility trainers. It requires following a number of sequential steps and using a variety of equipment; however, it is worth the trouble because it results in enthusiastic and reliable performances. In addition, dogs maintain their speed in the poles because they are never asked to slow down during the process.

Phase 1: Channels In this first step, the dog is taught to run between two sets of poles with an aisle or channel in between. The channel can be created by making two parallel lines of poles with space for the dog to run down the middle or by using commercial channel weaves built specifically for this process. The advantage of these channel weaves is that they are constructed so that the distance between the poles is twice as wide as competitive weaves. As the dog progresses and the poles are gradually scooted together, ultimately they mesh to become regulation width.

Teaching the Weave Poles

A target can be used to lure a dog down the channel.

1. When your channels are ready, have your partner hold your dog. Go to the far end and call your dog through the poles. Ideally, he will run to you, and you may reinforce with a treat or toy. If your dog has a tendency to duck out of the aisle and run around the outside of the poles, put him on a leash and walk him down the center until he gets the drill. Then, try calling him through the channels again. This activity should be repeated many times, generally over several weeks.

2. As you did with the jumps, your next step is to practice running with your dog as he goes through the channel. Hold your dog by the collar with him lined up with the channel. When he is looking at the obstacle, let go and move forward. Move parallel to your dog and stay even with his head. If your dog curves out of the poles to join you, you can set a target just beyond the channel or have your partner crouch at the exit with a target and treat. Make sure that you practice running an equal number of times on both sides of the poles, because it is very important that your dog be comfortable weaving on both your right and left.

3. The third step is to send your dog through the channel until he becomes comfortable driving ahead of you. Let your dog see you put his target or toy beyond the channel. Walk him back to the beginning, and release him as you did in the previous step. Hold

Training for Agility

back a bit as he runs through. As he exits, run forward to play with him, or reinforce his behavior with a treat. If he is hesitant to move ahead of you, put a treat on the target initially and then fade it out.

4. When your dog is comfortably and consistently running down the channel, scoot the poles in very gradually until they brush the dog's shoulders. If your dog starts coming out of the channel, widen the poles again until he is once again consistent about running down the aisle. Then narrow the channel very slowly. Remember, this process should take weeks or even months.

Phase 2: Offset Channels With Guides

When your dog can push through a very narrow channel with the poles brushing both of his shoulders, you are ready to move to Phase 2. At this level, your dog will actually weave. The poles, however, will be offset. This means they should be set up slightly staggered so that the dog can see them easily and so that he does not have to bend too much to get through. If you are using commercial channels or poles set in the ground, move the two lines together until the poles are almost, but not quite, lined up.

In addition to moving the poles closer together, it is wise to add some type of guide to the poles in this phase. The guides serve not only to keep the dog moving forward but also to teach him to bend around the poles. For dogs who duck out of the channel repeatedly, the guides can be added earlier. While some trainers worry that lengthy use of

The channel consists of two parallel lines of poles with space for the dog to run down the middle.

Teaching the Weave Poles

Guide wires allow a dog to run through the poles without making a mistake.

the guides makes a dog dependent on them, I believe they are the best tool that has been developed for agility. The guides allow the dog to blast through the poles without making a mistake that needs to be fixed later. I believe that Tucker, Scout, and Grace are immensely confident and fast in the poles because they were never asked to slow down or be careful.

Several options are available for guides. Clothesline wire looped around alternating poles on each side is not pretty, but it does work. Irrigation drip hose can be cut into sections and wired on the ends to make a loop that slips tightly over the poles. Varieties of commercial wire guides also are available that clip on and off the weave poles.

Tucker the Pap learned to master spectacular poles with only the clothesline guides. Scout the Sheltie and Grace the Corgi both started with a commercial set of guides made from wire mesh approximately 3 inches (7.62 cm) wide. They were highly visible. When each dog was comfortable weaving with those, I transitioned to both the irrigation hose guides and single-wire guides.

The following are instructions on how to teach your dog to maneuver the weave poles using guides:

1. When your poles are in place and your guides are on, hold your dog by the collar near the entry to the poles. Guide him into the poles, but release the collar as soon as he is within the wires.

2. Move forward parallel to the poles in a position directly across from his head. If he stays in the weaves, offer reinforcement in the form of a treat or toy a few feet (meters) beyond the end of the poles.

3. If your dog jumps out of the wires, respond neutrally. Take him back around and try again. If he jumps out again, put him on lead and take him through with support until he is successful. After a try or two at that, take him off lead and try it again.

4. When your dog is entering the poles confidently, stop holding the collar and let him find the entry when you give the command. Gradually move farther and farther back from the poles so that he learns to find the entry from a distance.

New Developments in Teaching Weave Poles

Teaching weave poles is the research and development branch of agility. Trainers are constantly developing and trying new methods to teach dogs to weave at high speed. Two newer approaches appear worthy of interest. The first, known as the *2 x 2 method*, teaches dogs to negotiate two poles at a time before the next two are added. Proponents maintain that it teaches the dogs not only to do the poles but also to understand the whole exercise. The second, called *shaping the weaves*, uses a target stick to lure the dogs quickly through the poles. Either of these methods might be appropriate for your dog, but both are highly specialized and require work with an experienced trainer. Even though I have more than a decade of agility training experience, I would not attempt to do these methods unaided.

Phase 3: Straight Poles With Guides When your dog consistently negotiates the offset poles with guides at top speed, he is ready for you to push the poles together so they are completely straight. The guides should remain on.

1. Because the poles will now be less visible to your dog, you may need to go back to helping him find the entry by holding his collar and guiding him in. As soon as he is comfortable, let go and allow him to enter the poles on his own.

2. At this stage, you can begin asking more of your dog. Practice approaching the poles from a variety of angles. Weave pole entries at agility courses have become more and more challenging in recent years, and dogs must understand that they should actively look for the correct space between the first two poles.

3. Remember to help your dog look straight ahead. A dog who turns his head toward you will miss poles when the wires are removed or pull out of the poles entirely. Encourage a forward focus by setting a target several feet (meters) beyond the end of the poles or tossing your toy just as the dog completes the poles. Experiment with your timing so that the toss encourages the dog to hurry forward but not to jump over the guides. Some dogs who are obstacle-focused will look forward if you place a jump beyond the weave poles.

Weave Pole Distances

Regulation weave poles are spaced between 18 (45.7 cm) and 24 inches (61.0 cm) apart. For training purposes, 21 (53.3 cm) to 22 inches (55.9 cm) is recommended.

Phase 4: Straight Poles The final step is to wean the dog from using the guides. Do this by taking off one guide at a time. It generally works best to remove a guide in the middle of the poles first and then remove them one at a time toward each end. On the weaves, young dogs make most mistakes at the entries and exits.

1. When working with a young dog who has been using guides and who appears to be ready to graduate to the next level, run him through the poles with guides a couple of times as a warm-up.

2. Then, without any fuss, take off one guide in the middle and run your dog through. He probably won't even notice that it's gone. That is a good sign.

3. Over the next several practices, put one of the wires on and take it off in an effort to make each repetition successful. Rotate the wire that is removed so that your dog doesn't know exactly what to expect.

4. If your dog does make a mistake and duck out where the wire is missing, try it one more time. Never allow him to make a mistake more than twice, however, before putting the guides back on, because dogs quickly pattern on doing the weaves incorrectly.

5. During subsequent weeks, take the guides off one at a time, then two at a time, and then three at a time until the only guides left are at the entry and exit. Leave these on until your dog is very consistent at finding the entry and staying in the poles until the very end.

Remember, if your dog backslides at any stage of the process, you should replace the guides before he makes multiple errors. Scout the Sheltie required a single guide at the exit for literally months after she knew the rest of the poles. On the other hand, the extra time invested in supporting her has led to a very consistent weave-pole performance.

Handling the Weave Poles

As a handler, you must remember a number of important things to help your dog with the weaves. First, give your dog the

---

Agility Speak

Some dogs are said to be *obstacle-focused*. These dogs assertively look for an obstacle to perform, often forgetting to check in with their handler. Other dogs are said to be *handler-focused*. This type of dog tends to rely on the handler to tell him everything to do. The best agility dogs are those capable of making lightning-fast shifts between a focus on the obstacles and a focus on the handler. This skill requires many months of working together.

Training for Agility

Weave Pole Practice

It is possible to train an agility dog without owning agility equipment—except when it comes to the weave poles. This obstacle requires *daily* training. If you practice this obstacle only once or twice a week at class, you may have a geriatric dog before you ever get to trial. Two or three short, daily training sessions with the weaves will help your dog make good progress.

Even with an athletic and willing dog, the weave pole process often takes many months. Take your time and enjoy the game. The day your dog clearly clicks with the poles may be one of the happiest days of your life.

command for this obstacle clearly and early. The weaves are not easy for the dog to see. It is common for beginning handlers to wait too long and to give a single command when the dog is just a few feet (meters) away from the first pole. This guarantees that your dog will not be able to collect himself to make the entry. Second, when your dog is in position to enter the poles, slow down. Let your dog find the entry while you hang back. If you keep charging forward, it is highly likely that your dog will come with you and miss the weave-pole entry.

Once your dog has made the entry, move forward quickly and position yourself across from your dog's head. If you stay behind your dog, he will likely turn his head to see where you are and miss a pole. If you forge ahead of your dog, he is likely

to come out of the poles to catch up. Stay right there until he exits the poles. One trick to help yourself stay with your dog rather than taking off for the next obstacle is to imagine there are 14 poles instead of 12. Don't run, change the length of your stride, pull away from your dog, or even twitch until the dog has had time to finish all 14.

Tucker the Pap made an honest woman of me at the weave poles. If I made any unexpected movement, he popped out. We missed qualifying on a standard run at the AKC Nationals as the result of my microscopic shoulder twitch that pulled him out at the 10th pole. When I remember to relax, breathe, and stay right across from his head right to the end, he weaves as fast as the best.

Last, some people help their dogs learn the weaves by doing an exaggerated swaying step to cue the dog to go back and forth through the poles. They step toward the dog to push him out and then away from the dog to pull him back. Dogs become dependent on this very quickly, and the handler is stuck looking like a dance class dropout. When training the weave poles, travel in a path parallel to your dog with your arms at your sides.

Caution

In the early days of agility, trainers taught their dogs to do the weave poles slowly and then tried to speed them up. This did not work. Once dogs learn the weaves are a slow, methodical activity, it is very challenging to change that mindset. From the first day that you begin teaching the weaves, then, make sure that your dog performs the exercises as fast as he can run. If he slows down while practicing the weaves, stop training and consider a different method.

Delivering Rewards

One additional handler issue—delivering treats and toys—requires a bit of an explanation. I notice some trainers stop to give their dog a reward immediately after the 12th pole when the dog does weaves correctly. Pretty soon, the dog begins to anticipate the reward and develops a habit of pulling out of the poles early. The reward intended to reinforce correct behavior becomes a problem. To avoid this issue, you can do one of two simple things: Either run 8 (2.4 m) or 10 feet (3.0 m) beyond the poles before you stop to reinforce the behavior, or ask the dog to do an obstacle such as a jump after the poles, and then deliver your treat or toy.

Generalizing From the Poles

Dogs do not generalize well. They frequently learn a behavior in one location, but in a different place, act as if they have never done it before. This is true of agility obstacles, too, but particularly of the weave poles. Grace the Corgi took quite a few months to learn the poles at home, and then, even though she had them nailed in her yard, it took a number of weeks before she was able to complete the poles in class without help from the guides. Be careful that you don't fall into the trap of thinking that your dog "knows" the poles and then getting grumpy if he isn't perfect everywhere. Dogs will pick up on your displeasure and react in a variety of ways, including slowing down.

While a dog is weaving, the handler should be positioned across from his head.

Training for Independence

It is important to teach the weave poles slowly and methodically and to use consistent body language in handling pole practice.

154

Training for Agility

Interestingly, there is a downside to that: Our consistency can foster a dog's dependency on our behaving exactly the same way each time.

The result is an interesting phenomenon. As novice dogs become reliable in performing the poles, handlers gradually begin to change their behavior, such as moving ahead of the dog, reaching in their pockets for a treat, or raising their hands to toss a toy while the dog is still weaving. The dogs, trained on consistency, respond by starting to make mistakes in the weaves.

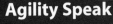

Agility Speak

When a handler stops to let a dog perform an obstacle, this is called *setting anchor*. It is particularly import to *set anchor* just behind the first pole while your dog finds the entry. If you keep moving, the dog is very likely to follow you. On the other hand, sometimes it is better to keep moving. Your dog will be able to find you more easily when coming out of a tunnel if you are moving toward the next obstacle.

Your dog can be trained to perform the poles independently and ignore your distracting behaviors if you choose to teach that. Start by putting the weave pole guide wires back on. If you did not train with them initially, let the dog run through several times to get used to the feeling and look of the wires. The wires will help the dog keep weaving while you begin to do the things I mentioned. You might also try changing your stride, twitching your shoulders, and taking one step away from the poles. If your dog completes the poles despite your behaviors, jackpot that behavior. He will gradually learn to perform the weaves independent of your actions because he understands his job.

Teach the weave poles slowly, and use consistent body language.

Teaching the Weave Poles

Chapter Fifteen

Handling Skills

Agility handling is the fine art of steering your dog through an agility course, using both verbal commands and body language. Learning to be an accomplished handler in this sport takes energy, commitment, and a willingness to look just plain silly on occasion.

Handlers, no matter how advanced, never quit learning new techniques to communicate with their dogs and to complete the course more efficiently.

If you have ever participated in other activities such as dance or a competitive sport, you will find that those skills and body awareness will translate to agility. If agility is the first sport you undertake with your dog, be ready to learn how to use your entire body from head to toe to help your dog understand where to go next.

Verbal Commands Versus Body Language

On an agility course, handlers tell their dogs which obstacle to do next. Verbal commands might sound like, "*Go over, here, get in, turn,*

Dogs follow body language more than verbal commands.

climb." The monologue is a combination of directional commands such as *here*, which means veer toward me, and the name of the obstacle, such as *climb*, which tells the dog to run over the A-frame. In the sequence above, the dog has been directed to go over a jump, run through a tunnel, and make a turn away from the handler to complete the A-frame.

Let me say once again that in agility, verbal commands are much less important than in other dog sports. Many would say that less than ten percent of a dog's performance in agility is based on what the handler says. The speed of agility limits the impact of verbal commands. A dog running full speed may complete 15 to 20 obstacles in about a minute and cannot hear and process the words fast enough to rely on them.

If it's not language that steers the dog, what does? The answer is the handler's body movement. The way your feet point, the way you turn, the degree to which you raise or drop your shoulders, and even where you are looking will have a much greater impact on where your dog goes than what you say. Body language works particularly well with dogs, because they have terrific peripheral vision. Even when you lag behind, your dog can see you and pick up on what you are communicating with your posture and movements.

Many novices fall into the trap of thinking that their dogs are following their verbal cues in agility much more than they actually are. You can test this. Once your dog is familiar with a few obstacles, run with intent at one of the obstacles, but give your dog the wrong command for the obstacle. I can almost guarantee that your dog will cue off of your movement, perform the obstacle, and ignore the word.

Agility Speak

Going *off course* means that your dog takes the incorrect obstacle in the sequence that you are performing. Depending on the organization, an occasional *off course* is allowed at the novice level. At the intermediate and advanced levels, an *off course* results in disqualification.

This concept is very important to grasp if you want a speedy canine partner. Handlers who rely heavily on verbal commands inadvertently slow their dogs down. Unsure where to go next, the dog has to slow down to hear the words. Gradually, the handler has a dog who waits to be escorted around the course. The point of agility is to have a dog who is an eager partner, actively looking for the next obstacle and reading your body language to select the correct one. If you learn to use your movements to communicate clearly with your dog, and your dog learns to understand this communication, you not only will have more success but a great deal more fun as a team.

This doesn't mean you should quit talking. Occasionally, a strong *"Come, come, come weave"* may be just what you need to turn your dog away from an incorrect obstacle and toward the correct obstacle. But those words will have much greater power if your feet and shoulders turn, too.

One last point about what distinguishes the sport of agility: Handlers can and should use commands as many times as needed. Unlike competitive obedience, where one is limited to a single direction such as "Stanley, heel," there are no limits on repetition in agility. On tight turns or in places where the dog must be called away from the wrong obstacle, repeating commands and the dog's name is both acceptable and effective. One highly successful national competitor with a high-drive Golden Retriever is known for her trademark yell, "Ted, Ted, Ted" when she needs to get him back on course.

Learning to Use Body Language

In this overview, we'll work from top to bottom as I review what body movements you can use to communicate with your dog.

Watch Your Dog

Before we take a look at specific body language, it is important to mention one of the most important skills that you, as a handler, must acquire and maintain in agility training: watching your dog at all times.

From the beginning of your training, develop a habit of keeping your eye on your dog from the start to the finish line. Since you will both be running full speed, you will have to use your peripheral vision. The minute you lose sight of your dog, it is highly likely that your dog will take the wrong obstacle. Accomplished trainers are so good at watching their dogs, they are able to tell what their dogs are looking at and stop an off-course before it happens.

Eyes

While you are watching your dog, he is watching you. In fact, your dog can see where you are looking. Seriously. It is important that you look at the obstacle you want him to perform next. If you are looking around to see where to go, there is a good chance he will go off course.

Shoulders

Shoulders are a powerful communication tool, particularly for medium and big dogs. Seasoned handlers use their shoulders in two ways. First, a turn of the shoulders in either direction is used to communicate a turn in that direction. The degree of shoulder rotation indicates how sharp the turn is to the dog. Second, a drop in one shoulder is used to tell the dog that the handler is going to rear cross. (More about this move in a moment.)

Arms

Below are three basic ways to use your arms to train your dog. Your dog will learn to recognize what these signals mean as you train together.

Bowling Your Dog Your primary communication with your dog is done with the arm closest to him. If your dog is on your right, your right arm will steer, and if your dog is on the left, then your left arm should go to work. There are times when the other arm will come into play, but only as you become an advanced handler.

Training for Agility

The palm should be face up on whatever arm is working. By swinging this arm toward the next obstacle, you can quickly tell the dog where to go. Some people refer to this movement as "bowling the dog"—a good image when you are getting started.

Not all bowling motions are created equal. Rather than a loose, flopping arm, bowl your dog with a strong, controlled motion. Remember, your dog does not know where to go next, so make your motions simple and clear.

The hand closest to the dog should "bowl" him onto the correct obstacle.

Drawing a Path

As you gain confidence, the communication with your working arm can get more sophisticated. Rather than using your arm only to swing back and forth, you can begin to move it so that you actually show your dog the correct path. For example, your arm may curve away from you to show your dog that he needs to turn away, or it may come across your body to pull him toward you. At this stage, many handlers actually point with one finger and see themselves drawing their dog's path on the ground.

Use your finger to draw a path for your dog.

Pushing the Dog Away Sometimes a course is set up so that you can't run right up to the obstacle with your dog. This is one situation in which your *go on* command comes into play. In addition to your verbal command, you can use your body language to push the dog away from

To "push" your dog, use an open palm as if you were shoving him away.

Handling Skills

you in the direction of the obstacle.

To "push" your dog, turn your open palm toward him and use a pushing motion, which will look exactly as if you were shoving him toward the obstacle. There is no real contact, of course.

Feet

Your feet are immensely important in handling, whatever the size of your canine partner. Many small dog handlers swear that their dogs cue mainly off their feet, but all dogs learn to "read" your feet like the arrow on a compass.

The rule about feet is simple: Your feet should face the next obstacle as soon as possible. For example, if you have sent your dog into a tunnel, and the next obstacle is the dogwalk, your feet should be directly pointed at the dogwalk when your dog reappears.

Changing Position

In addition to using eyes, arms, and feet to communicate with their dogs, handlers also tell the dog where to go on a course by changing position in relation to the dog. The handler may leave the dog in a *stay* briefly, switch sides, or move farther off to the side of the dog. Those of you with a background in dance will have a distinct advantage in executing these moves. Here are the three most common moves.

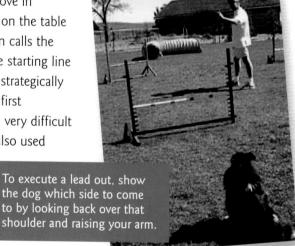

Lead Out The lead out is an agility move in which the dog is left at the start line or on the table while the handler moves ahead and then calls the dog to her. This maneuver is used at the starting line so that the handler can position herself strategically on the course and call her dog over the first obstacle(s). Advanced courses are often very difficult without a good lead out. This move is also used when the dog is staying on the table during the judge's five-second count, to help the handler get a good start on the next obstacle.

To execute a lead out, show the dog which side to come to by looking back over that shoulder and raising your arm.

Training for Agility

To execute a lead out, here are the steps:

1. Go to the desired spot on the course.
2. Point your feet at the next obstacle you want your dog to perform.
3. If you want the dog to come to your right side, rotate your right shoulder back toward your dog. Extend your right arm back toward your dog with your palm up. Look at your dog over your shoulder. If you want your dog to come to your left side, turn to your left and extend your left arm.
4. Use your *release* command to call your dog over the obstacle(s).
5. As your dog approaches, use your bowling motion to indicate the next obstacle and start moving in the desired direction, stepping first with the foot closest to your dog. It is important not to close your shoulders (turn them forward) or turn your back on your dog too quickly, because this will give him a choice to come up on either side of you, and you may lose sight of him.

Clearly, a lead out requires your dog to stay while you move away. Keep your lead outs short at first, so that your dog can be successful. Over time, it's ideal to have the ability to lead out past several obstacles. If you are still working on a solid *stay*, you can practice your lead outs by having your partner hold your dog until you call.

Front Cross The front cross is a maneuver that allows the handler to change the dog's direction and to change the side on which the dog is working. The front cross is a "must-have" skill for agility handlers. The front cross is accomplished by rotating in front of your dog on course, always keeping the front of your body facing your dog. During a front cross, you never lose sight of your dog or turn your back to him. The front cross is effective because the rotation of your body tells the dog clearly that a change is coming, while allowing you to keep your eyes on him.

To the right is a map of what the front cross looks like. On the map, the solid line represents the dog's path, and the dotted line represents the

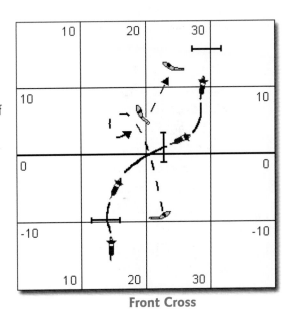

Front Cross

Handling Skills

Caution

Most people who become involved in agility are clear that it is just a great way to have fun with dogs. Then, something happens to many people and they get serious. Suddenly, earning titles becomes important. As a result, they put pressure on themselves, and worse, on their dogs.

The most successful handlers are remarkably even tempered. They know that there is always another trial and another run. Their dogs never know when they are disappointed. As you become more involved in agility, strive to keep the sport simple and fun.

handler's path. Note that in this case, the handler is starting with the dog on her left, and her goal is to end up with the dog on her right. When the cross is completed, the handler is said to have "picked the dog up on the right hand." This simply means that the left hand gave the directions before the cross but, after the cross, the right hand showed the dog what to do next.

To perform the front cross shown on this map:

Handlers must be able to front cross in both directions.

1. Move ahead of your dog in a lateral position (off to the side). This action may require sending your dog to an obstacle and cutting the corner. Note the position of the handler on the map.
2. Turn toward your left hand to face your dog.
3. Keep turning smoothly to your left until you are facing the desired direction. Pick up your dog on your right hand.
4. Move forward toward the next obstacle with the dog now on the right.

Above left, from top:

To perform a front cross, first move ahead and off to the side of your dog.

Turn toward your left hand to face your dog, and drop your left arm. (Note that the handler in this photo is drawing a path for her dog.)

Keep turning smoothly, and pick up your dog on your right hand.

Move forward to the next obstacle with your dog now on your right.

Training for Agility

When you start with the dog by your right hand, remember to turn toward your right hand. Your goal is to end up with the dog on your left side without turning your back on your dog. Keep turning until you can pick the dog up on your left hand.

The front cross presents two challenges. Getting ahead of a fast dog requires very quick feet and the ability to work laterally—that is, a good distance off to the side of the dog. If you have to run right up to each obstacle with your dog, the front cross will be very difficult. The second challenge is that the handler must keep moving forward while turning. The tendency is to spin in place rather than move toward the next obstacle in the sequence. Spinning in place tends to make you dizzy, and you will end up behind your dog, which makes it difficult to handle subsequent obstacles.

The best way to master this move is to practice at home without your dog. Find a good space, picture your imaginary dog, and do the front cross dance. Check that you are turning so that you can "see" your imaginary dog through your whole turn and that you are both turning and moving forward.

Rear Cross The rear cross is a second maneuver that allows you to change the dog's direction and the side on which the dog is working. The rear cross is accomplished by sending the dog over an obstacle, sliding across to the other side while the dog performs the obstacle, and picking the dog up on the opposite hand. For example, on the map to the right, the handler sent her dog to a jump with her left hand, slid across behind the jump once the dog was committed to jumping, and picked up the dog on the right hand as the dog landed. She is now in the correct position to show the dog both the second and third jumps. The solid line represents the dog's path, and the dotted line represents the handler's path.

To perform the rear cross shown on this map:

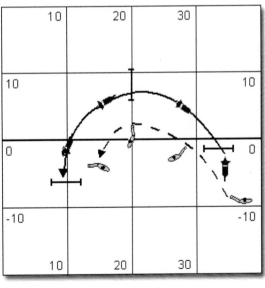

Rear Cross

Handling Skills

1. Run with your dog to the first obstacle, building up as much speed as possible.
2. As you near the jump, drop your shoulder closest to the dog, and use your arm to show the dog the obstacle. With practice, this will serve as a cue to your dog that a cross is coming.
3. As your dog commits to the jump, move smoothly across to the opposite side.
4. Drop your left hand and pick up your dog on your right hand.
5. Keep moving smoothly toward the next obstacle.

The rear cross works very well with high-drive dogs; however, it can be difficult with slower dogs who slam to a halt when they see their handler start to switch sides. Low-drive dogs can be trained to tolerate the rear cross if, during practice, the handler tosses a toy or food bag over the jump just as the handler crosses. This keeps the dog's attention forward rather than back.

One variation on the traditional rear cross is the *landing-side rear cross*. In this maneuver, the handler waits until the dog completes the obstacle, then ducks behind him very quickly and picks him up on the opposite hand. The advantage of the landing-side rear cross is that is you won't earn a refusal if your dog hesitates in front of the obstacle. The disadvantage is that it can be slower than the other rear cross and often makes the dog spin. To the right is a diagram of this move.

Although these maps show jumps only, agility handlers front and rear cross at virtually every obstacle. Tunnels are a great place for a rear cross, because the dog doesn't see you change sides, but experienced handlers also rear cross at the weave poles or dogwalk. The two-on/two-off contact allows you to front cross if necessary at the bottom of the contact obstacles. The only thing you should be cautious about is a rear cross at a triple or double jump. Dogs often knock bars on the big jumps if the handler moves across.

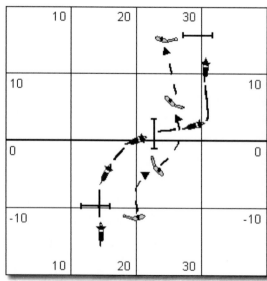

Landing-Side Rear Cross

Training for Agility

Agility Speak

In some agility venues, judges may penalize a team for a *refusal*, which means that the dog, once he has seen an obstacle, has stopped his forward motion, however briefly. Even if refusals are not penalized, they use up extra seconds. Smooth handling and clear communication will help you avoid refusals.

Timing

Knowing what to do with your body to steer your dog is one thing; knowing when to do it is another. Exquisite timing of verbal commands and body language separates the good agility handler from the great agility handler. Perfect timing results when a handler knows her dog's strengths and weaknesses and possesses the skills to communicate quickly in a way that that particular dog understands. Some dogs must be directed to the next obstacle very early. Speedy Scout the Sheltie will tear off course if she is jumping, and I haven't told her what to do next, particularly if the tunnel Sirens are calling. Other dogs will knock bars if the handler talks to them while they are jumping. If I open my mouth while Grace the Corgi is airborne, her back legs drop, and the bar comes down. Learning the timing that is correct for *your* dog is part of the agility adventure.

In general, the biggest challenge for novices is cueing the dog in time for the dog to react. It is common to see newer handlers tell their dogs to weave only a few feet (meters) in front of the poles or to jump when the dog is almost on top of the obstacle. A good rule is to cue sooner than you think you should, using your body and verbal commands.

Above right, from top:

To perform a rear cross, when running toward the obstacle, drop your shoulder closest to your dog and indicate the obstacle with your arm.

As your dog commits to the jump, move smoothly across to the other side

Handling Skills

Handling on Both Sides

Agility dogs must work on both sides equally well. I mentioned this earlier, but it bears repeating in a world where heeling means working on the left side only. Dogs adjust easily to the idea of working on both sides, but humans sometimes find it challenging to be agility ambidextrous. As you learn the moves discussed in this chapter, make sure to practice everything on your right *and* left sides.

Toys

Early in the book, I mentioned the importance of teaching your dog to play with you. One of your essential jobs as a handler is to keep your dog excited and motivated to play the agility game. This is where your toys come in.

You can use your dog's favorite toy in a variety of ways. First, use the toy to get the dog warmed up and excited before class or a trial run. You will see many top handlers playing tug with their dog right before their turn in the ring. Scout the Sheltie loves to wrestle over her Frisbee before we start a class or a trial. Next, use your toy to reinforce a good performance. If your dog makes the tight turn you ask for in class, pull that toy out of your pocket and play. When he pushes through the chute, let him find you with his toy, ready for a game. Last, use your toy as a training tool. For example, toss the toy over a jump while you rear cross. Tucker the Pap, who is fanatical about small tennis balls, was easily taught to let me rear cross by throwing the ball over the jump just before I switched sides. He will perform virtually every obstacle at warp speed if there is a chance his toy will appear.

With toys, the tendency exists to use them only at the end of a sequence or practice run in class. Thus, as a dog learns to perform more obstacles, he gets less frequent reinforcement. This slows down low-drive dogs. From day one until the end of your dog's agility career, use your toy as an element of surprise. Play with your dog after one obstacle, three obstacles, seven obstacles, or anywhere on course.

Breaking the Rules

In competition, handlers are not allowed to do a couple of things. First, you can't touch or push your dog in any way that appears to aid the dog's performance. If the judge thinks this has happened, even if it was not intentional, the team is disqualified. If the physical contact has little influence on the run, the judge usually ignores it. Second, you can't do anything to the dog that the judge believes is harsh, whether it is verbal discipline or inappropriate physical contact. Obviously, it's a subjective call, but fortunately, most judges have little tolerance for anything that might reflect badly on the sport or discourage the dog. Last of all, handlers can't

Exquisite timing of verbal commands and body language to communicate with a dog distinguish outstanding handlers.

knock down any obstacles. I speak from personal experience when I say it is not uncommon for handlers to clip jumps.

Mistakes

Agility is a fast, fun, and complex sport. Both dogs and people get excited. Obstacles are missed. Dogs race out of the ring to kiss a photographer. Handlers forget the course. However, the bottom line is simple: When something goes wrong in agility, *it is always the handler's fault.*

This seems so simple an idea, but when people become competitive, their egos get involved. Sometimes they get embarrassed. If you do nothing else, remember that agility is just a game. Your dog doesn't know the course. He doesn't care about ribbons or titles. He just cares about playing with you. Never let him know you are disappointed, because he will pick up even the most subtle tones of unhappiness in your voice.

One of the best handlers in the United States has a simple rule. He enters every course with a single goal: to ensure that his dog has the most fun he can have. This philosophy has brought him several national championships. Take care to have the most fun you can on every run with your dog.

Chapter Sixteen

Sequencing

I t is wonderful when your dog understands how to perform correctly at least some of the obstacles, and you can begin teaching him to do several obstacles in a row, one after another. Sequencing is what agility is ultimately all about. The process begins with two or three obstacles, and then more are added, one at a time, until the dog can run a full-length agility course.

Readiness

Before we look at beginning sequences, there is one extremely important consideration— readiness. When people initially become involved in agility, they are often excited about the prospect of running whole courses, and a tendency exists to start sequencing too soon or to run sequences that are too long for the dog's development. The consequence is that the dogs develop bad habits that are hard to correct, or they get turned off because the demands are too high.

I recently received an e-mail from a woman whose pre-novice Silky Terrier had started out very enthusiastically in agility, but after a couple of months of going to class, she had stopped running altogether. When I asked more about the class, the handler said that they ran courses of 15 or more obstacles. I suggested that she find another class, where her dog would be asked to do only a couple of obstacles and then would receive plenty of positive reinforcement. She did exactly that, and her dog's enthusiasm is starting to come back.

I would suggest that you use three criteria to decide when your dog is ready to move from performing individual obstacles to short sequences:

You should only begin to sequence when your dog can perform the obstacles you want to sequence at a high level, when he plays the agility game as fast as he can, and when he has mastered the basic obedience commands.

1. **He can perform the obstacles you want to sequence at a high level.** For example, a contact should not be included unless you *know* your dog will stop on the contact. A closed tunnel should not be used unless the dog is assertively pushing through the chute. A tunnel can be included if your dog enthusiastically runs into the tunnel while you are several feet (meters) away, and he can find the tunnel entry from a variety of angles.

2. **He plays the agility game as fast as he can.** Although not every dog is a speed demon, your dog should be performing single obstacles with enthusiasm before you start asking him to do a series of obstacles.

3. **He has mastered the basic obedience commands.** For example, if your dog runs away from you, stops to sniff, or skips obstacles consistently, he is not ready to sequence.

Training for Agility

Basic Guidelines

It is not necessary for your dog to know all the obstacles before he begins to sequence. The easier obstacles, such as the jumps, table, and open tunnel, make exciting sequences for dogs in the early stages of agility training if they are structured correctly.

Here are some of the basic guidelines for teaching your dog to sequence:

- Keep the sequences short and easy so that your dog is fast and successful.
- Do only straight-line sequences initially. Curves will come later.
- Set the jumps very low. There is no need for your dog to worry about jumping high initially.
- Work with your dog on either side of you so that he is equally relaxed with you in either position. This will matter later, when the obstacles are curved
- Follow the training pattern you used for the obstacles. First, call your dog over the sequence. Then, run with your dog. Finally, send him through the sequence.

Agility Speak

Sequencing is the process of teaching a dog to perform two or more obstacles in a series. Sequences for novice dogs typically include two or more jumps, a jump and a tunnel, or a jump to the table. The goal in agility is to train a dog to complete sequences of up to 20 obstacles with speed and enthusiasm.

You or your partner should be at the end of each sequence, luring the dog forward in a straight line.

- Use your tab leash, as discussed earlier. A long leash can easily tangle during a sequence and trip or scare your dog.
- Include only the obstacles that your dog can perform at a high level. (This is a point worth repeating!)
- Work with a partner.

A training partner is ideal during the first weeks of sequencing. You or your partner should be at the end of each sequence, luring the dog forward in a straight line. For example, if you start with a sequence such as a jump, an open tunnel, and then the table, one of you should stand behind the table and call the dog to keep him running forward. This is very important, because dogs want to naturally curve toward the handler; they have to be taught to drive straight ahead.

Beginner Sequences

Two sequences are perfect to use with novice dogs. The first is the one mentioned above. The second sequence is just three jumps in a line. Start with the jumps about 15 feet (4.6 m) apart.

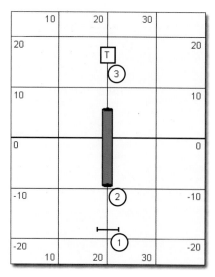

Beginner Sequence #1

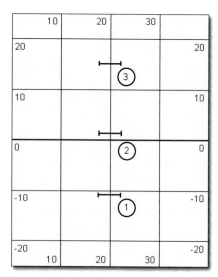

Beginner Sequence #2

Training for Agility

Teaching Your Dog to Sequence

The following steps will help you and your dog learn to sequence:

1. To begin work on either Beginner Sequence #1 or Beginner Sequence #2, position yourself behind Obstacle 3 (the table or jump). You should have a delectable treat or a favorite toy.

2. Have your friend walk your dog out to "see" the treat, and then run him back behind Obstacle 2.

3. Ask your friend to let your dog go while you call him to you. Chances are good that he will take the two obstacles if he has done enough groundwork. If he does, praise and reward him. Don't ask for a *sit* or *down* on the table. Just be pleased if he gets on. Practice Obstacles 2 and 3 this same way several times.

4. Next, have your friend take your dog behind Obstacle 1. Repeat the process with you calling your dog. If he takes all three obstacles, praise and reward him. Repeat the exercise over several sessions until your dog is comfortable.

5. Next, switch spots. Put your friend behind obstacle 3. This time, you should take your dog behind the second obstacle, release, and run with him. Have your friend call your dog to keep him running straight.

   5a. You may notice more of a tendency from your dog to curve toward you than you did when you were doing the calling. This may make him miss an obstacle. To address this, make sure that your friend has something really, really exciting to draw the dog's attention forward. (It may be time to bring out the barbecued chicken bits.)

   5b. Also, make sure that you don't say your dog's name or talk to him while he is doing the sequence.

6. When your dog is driving straight ahead over the two-obstacle sequence, add Obstacle 1 to make a three-obstacle sequence.

   6a. If your dog consistently ducks around one of the obstacles, which often happens with the three-jump sequence, you may need to do a bit of problem solving. Try setting the jumps very low (4 [10.2 cm] or 8 inches [20.3 cm]). Also, stop rewarding the dog at the end of the sequence if he has avoided a jump. Just ask kindly if he would like to go try it again, and when he gets it right, jackpot with a series of treats or a long game of tug.

   6b. If your dog is still ducking, you may need to adjust the distance between the obstacles. For a small dog, 10 (3.0 m) feet between obstacles may be just right to draw his attention, while a larger dog may easily handle 15 (4.6 m) feet in between. If these strategies don't help the dog to take all the jumps, go back to two jumps for a while.

7. When your dog takes the line of three jumps easily while you run with him, it's time to encourage him to run ahead of you. Position your training partner behind the final obstacle. As you release your dog behind the first obstacle, she should call your dog to keep him focused on running forward. This time, start to hang back a bit. Let your dog drive on ahead of you. This will encourage him to develop initiative and not be dependent on watching you every minute. Once he gets to or completes the final obstacle in the sequence, run out and lavish him with praise.

Using Your Toy (or Food Bag)

Remember when we talked about tossing a toy or a food-stuffed bag over an obstacle to get your dog to go ahead of you? You can use that same strategy on some sequences. When I have to work without a partner, I put my dog's favorite toy on the ground out beyond the last jump in the sequence, let him see it, walk him back by the tab to the beginning of the line of jumps, and let him go. In another practice session, I run with him but toss the toy or his food bag over the third jump.

Incorporating Your Lead Out

A three-obstacle sequence is the perfect time to start practicing a lead out that will get you in a good starting position on course.

1. Leave your dog on a *stay* behind the first obstacle. Make sure that he has enough room to jump.
2. Walk out between the first and second obstacles.
3. Release your dog and point at the first jump that you want him to take. As soon as he commits to jumping it, give him your command for the next obstacle, and off you go. Make sure to do this with your dog on both your right and left.

   3a. If your dog starts breaking his *stay* because he is excited to get playing, don't just ignore it. There is a strong tendency to do that because you want to do the sequence as much as he does. However, if you let him start breaking now, you will never have a reliable *stay*.

Caution

Some dogs become very excited when you start to sequence, and they may spin, bark, and even nip. Generally, the herding dogs are most prone to demonstrating these behaviors.

If your dog starts doing any of these things, work on giving your commands more quickly, so that he continues moving forward and doesn't have time to engage in these undesirable behaviors. Also, go back to shorter sequences, and only reward completion of the sequence without those behaviors. Add new obstacles very gradually, only when the previous level has been completed successfully.

3b. Stop moving the minute he gets up before you give his release word. Stand still as we discussed before. Let him come to you before you move. Don't talk to him. After he clearly recognizes that there is a problem, walk slowly back to the start. Ask him to sit nicely, and praise him when he does. Leave him and walk around the first obstacle, but return and reward while he stays. Do this several times. If he holds, give his release word and run the sequence.

Body Language

In Chapter 15, we discussed the importance of body language. Once you start to sequence, it is time to put it into action. Point your feet and shoulders at the obstacle you want your dog to take. Use a tidy bowling motion with your hand to show the correct obstacle.

Verbal Commands

Because your initial sequences are all straight lines, there is no need to get fancy. On Beginner Sequence #1, if you are running with your dog, just say, "Over, tunnel, table." If you have used a lead out, add your release word and say, "Okay, over, tunnel, table." On Beginner Sequence #2, it would be adequate to simply say, "Over, over, over."

Timing Your Commands

Once you begin sequencing, the timing of your commands is very important. On Beginner Sequence #1, it would be ideal to give your dog the tunnel command while he is in the air over the jump. Unfortunately, some dogs drop their legs when you talk and knock a bar. Learning the timing that works for your dog is something with which you will have to experiment, but in general, the rule is the earlier the better.

One of the things that newer handlers frequently slip into is giving verbal commands late. What this means is that the dog hears the command so late that he can't change what he is about to do. On straight-line sequences, you will get away with late commands because your dog is just taking the obvious obstacle. But later on, when you are doing complex courses, a late command will often result in your dog going off course, because he won't have time to adjust his path. It is important to practice giving early commands before you even need them.

Advanced Beginner Sequences

When your dog is successful performing the two straight-line sequences described earlier, (Beginner Sequence#1 and Beginner Sequence #2), create more difficult exercises by adding curves and turns. This is okay now, since your dog has learned how to run straight ahead when needed.

A curved path is challenging, because the dog must understand that he should run on the outside of the curve rather than ducking behind you and taking the shorter route. This is definitely a learned rather than a natural behavior.

You can evaluate whether your dog is ready to move to this level with a simple test. Put your dog on your right, and jog in a large circle (15- [4.6-m] to 20-foot [6.1-m] diameter) with you on the inside and your dog on the outside. Then try it going in the other direction. If your dog races along next to your outside hand, then you are ready to move to the advanced beginner level.

If your dog tries to duck into the inside of the circle or runs in front of you so that you might trip, take some time to practice this game until you can run together smoothly in a circle. Start by practicing with your dog on leash, and progress to running the circle with your dog off lead. This skill is the basis for many agility exercises.

When you are ready to go, set up three or four jumps on a curve, as shown. Put the jumps at a low height so that your dog isn't working hard to clear the jumps.

Training for Agility

Exercise #1

To complete this exercise, stand on the inside of the curve, and run with your dog as he takes the jumps. If the curve confuses him, break the exercise down by having him do just Jump 4, then 3 and 4, then 2 and 3 and 4. Then try all four jumps. If your dog gets confused and has trouble finding the next jump, it is a great time to toss your toy or food bag over the jump so that he sees where you want him to go. Then, run the circle in one direction with your dog taking all the jumps, reverse, and go the opposite way. Always end while your dog is successful.

Gradually move the jumps until they make a complete circle. This may take several practice sessions.

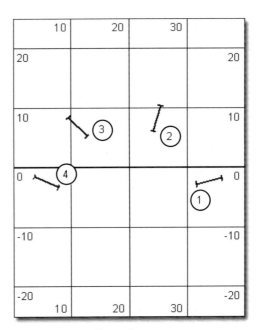

Exercise #1

Exercise #2

In this exercise, start your dog behind any of the jumps, and direct him around the circle. If he has learned the circle running game, he will catch on quickly. Toss your toy out over jumps at regular intervals to reward him for moving forward and taking the jump. Once your dog jumps around the entire circle easily, remember to try the reverse direction.

When your dog is comfortable and speedy with circle jumping, add other obstacles such as a tunnel and table to make the game a bit more complicated and fun.

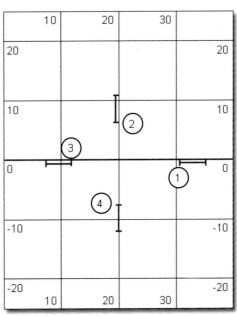

Exercise #2

Sequencing

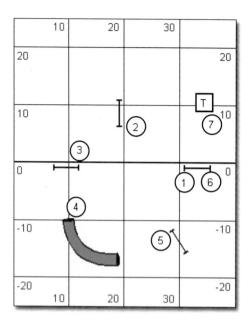

Exercise #3

Exercise #3

On this sequence, start with your dog at an angle so that he is on a line to Jump 2. This is important, because your dog could easily see the table and think that it is the correct obstacle after the first jump. (Remember that any obstacle may be used more than once in a sequence, as you see in this exercise.) After your dog clears Jump 6, make a serious effort to run even with his head so that you can use your body language to push him toward the table.

Exercise #4

Most sequences can be made more difficult by just throwing in a sophisticated handling move. For example, if you add a front cross anywhere on Exercise #3, it becomes considerably more challenging. Take a look at Exercise #4.

The most efficient way to run this sequence now is to front cross after Jump 2. (If you need a refresher on the front cross, review Chapter 15.)

Exercise #5

For those who are overachievers, here is one more sequence, this time with six weave poles. It also has a dummy jump, which is not part of the sequence, but it is put on course to test a dog's ability (with guidance from the handler) to discriminate between the correct and an incorrect obstacle.

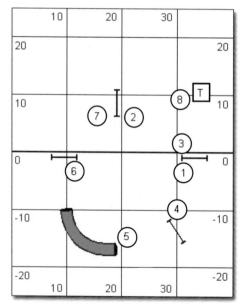

Exercise #4

Training for Agility

As you did with the previous exercise, front cross after Jump 2. After sending your dog over Jump 3, slow down a bit to help your dog locate the weave poles. If your dog is still using wires as a tool to learn how to weave, it is fine to use them in a sequence. Remember to turn your shoulders and feet toward Jump 7, so that your dog understands that he needs to remain on the curve rather than running forward toward the dummy jump. As your dog clears Jump 7, again try to align yourself with his head so that you can use your body language to direct him to the table.

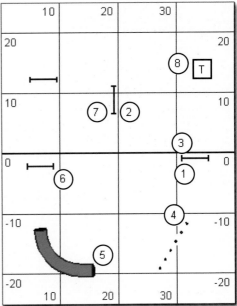

Exercise #5

Any time you encounter a sequence that is too hard for your dog, it is important to make it easier. Dogs can get easily discouraged if they are asked to do exercises that are beyond their current understanding of the agility game. The best way to help your dog is to break a sequence into sections. Then piece the sections together to do the whole exercise. For example, you could start Exercise #5 by doing Obstacles 1 through 4. Then do 5 through 8. If that goes well, put both parts together to run the whole exercise.

Once you acquire a few pieces of equipment, you can set up hundreds of different sequences on a backyard lawn. Just changing the angle on a jump or two will change the skills that you and your dog need.

Even when your dog starts to run substantial sequences, don't be afraid to go back and do short, high-energy sequences with lots of reinforcement. For example, after several long, challenging exercises at class, I start tossing Scout the Sheltie's toy after every three or four obstacles. She never knows when the toy will appear, and it keeps her excited and interested.

Chapter Seventeen

Training Challenges

Teaching your dog the obstacles and sequencing may not go completely smoothly. For most dogs, agility training is a mix of progress and setbacks. For example, your dog may start turning around and popping out of the tunnels he was running through the week before. He may suddenly be apprehensive about the dogwalk after running across it for weeks. He may prefer to herd the table rather than get on it.

When a dog suddenly refuses to perform something you thought he knew, it is tempting to think that he is "blowing you off" or "just being stubborn." When this conclusion is drawn, some trainers try to fix the problem by being stern—and that always makes the problem worse. You are sure to encounter challenges of some sort in agility training. Knowing that, be prepared to think creatively about other training methods, rather than thinking your dog is "broken."

Reasons for Training Setbacks

When a dog suffers a training setback, it is generally for one or more of the following reasons:

1. The dog may have become afraid of an obstacle. Something as simple as jamming a toenail while coming down the A-frame can make a sensitive dog worry about running down again.

2. The dog may have concluded not enough payoff is coming—playtime or treats—to keep performing. A dog who feels too much pressure or disappointment from the handler will simply shut down.

3. The dog may not have known how to do the exercise as well as the handler had assumed. Using positive problem solving is always the correct response when training is not progressing as you hoped.

It is not always clear what is bothering a dog. A friend's Golden Retriever mix had been terrific at the teeter. In his first novice trials, he would run nearly to the end of the board and stand firm while the teeter slammed down. Then one day, he started refusing to go up the teeter in class or at trials. Without knowing what had happened, the handler knew she needed to regain his confidence. She returned to basic teeter training, using a board flat on the ground

If you encounter a challenge when agility training, try to think creatively about other training methods that can help your dog succeed.

Training for Agility

and gradually raising it on one end, inches (centimeters) at a time. She took several months to retrain. The story had a happy ending: The dog now competes at the elite level in agility and shows no concern as he races up the teeter and rides it down.

You should also remember that certain groups and breeds of dog are prone to specific behaviors that do not constitute an issue until we ask them to do agility. Genes tell hunting dogs to circle and use their noses. Herding dogs may bark themselves silly during an agility run and nip at a handler who is not moving quickly enough. The sighthounds are capable of taking off after a blowing leaf. All of these challenges are surmountable with good training, but it's essential to spend extra time addressing the aspect of the sport that presents the greatest challenge to your dog. And always keep your sense of humor!

Common Training Issues

When your dog begins to have a problem with any part of the agility game, the first step is to rule out any physical problems that may be affecting your dog's behavior. A dog who becomes reluctant to jump may be experiencing neck problems. A "stubborn" dog may have hearing loss. A dog who takes several stutter steps before jumping may be having vision issues. Recently, a friend's dog who weaves so fast he bounces against the poles quit weaving. A visit to the vet revealed a broken tooth. Once the dental problem was corrected, a bit of retraining returned him to full form.

Dozens of other physical problems can affect a dog's performance. If your dog is struggling in any way, have your veterinarian give your canine partner a checkup. Once any physical problems are remedied or ruled out, you can head back to the agility course.

Here is a short list of the most common problems and what you might try. Remember that each dog is an individual and may respond best to a unique approach.

Popping Out of the Weave Poles

Dogs who know the weave poles one day frequently start popping out of them the next. A pop-out at the 10th pole is the most common issue. If this happens, try a dual solution.

First, reteach the poles. Return to the method that worked originally, such as guide wires or hand-in-the-collar method. While your dog is getting a refresher course, consider your handler behaviors that may have created the problem. Work on correcting your own handling before asking the dog to weave again without support.

Popping Out of the Weave Poles

Nine Nasty Handler Behaviors	How to Fix Them
Looks up to check the location of the next obstacle while the dog is still weaving.	Many people have changed this habit by picturing two imaginary poles beyond the real 12th pole. Stay with your dog and keep your head down until the dog passes the imaginary 14th pole.
Begins to praise the dog before he exits the poles.	Remain quiet until the dog's head starts to exit the last pole.
Plunges her hand into her pocket for a treat or toy	Keep those hands out in plain sight.
Raises her hand to throw a toy as reinforcement.	Keep that toy down until your dog exits.
Changes the rhythm of her walk, such as lengthening stride.	To check this out, it is helpful to get videotaped. If you are speeding up or shifting subtly away from the poles, work on maintaining the same pace and lateral distance
Changes or stops verbal cadence.	Either stick to the same cadence or lose it altogether. If it is a matter of running out of air, start speaking at the 3rd or 4th pole rather than at the 1st pole.
Gets too far ahead of the dog.	In general, you should stay aligned with your dog's head. Eventually, you will want to be able to move ahead for a front cross, but don't push this too hard too soon.
Gets too far behind the dog.	When the handler stays behind, the dog will tend to look back and miss the next pole. Again, in general, you should stay aligned with your dog's head.
Delivers rewards immediately after the 12th pole.	The best bet is to skip delivering any treat immediately after the poles. A dog who expects a treat here may start popping out in anticipation. Have your dog complete the poles and a subsequent obstacle, and then stop to reward. If you feel you must offer a treat after the poles, put a marker such as a cone several feet (meters) beyond the poles. Take your dog to that spot before you reward.

Pausing at the Top of the A-Frame

Some dogs love heights. They race up the A-frame and stop to survey their kingdom. While this is cute, it eats up precious seconds.

Training for Agility

To accelerate your dog's trip over this obstacle, lure him over the top with a treat or toy. Sweep your arm down the A-frame in front of your pup. Reinforce at the bottom of the obstacle.

Blowing Contacts

Failure to perform "good" contacts takes two separate forms. First, for handlers who have taught the two on/two off, a blown contact may mean that the dog didn't stop in the correct position with front feet on the grass and back feet on the obstacle. The dog may have touched the contact zone as he ran down, but he didn't succeed at performing the expected behavior. Second, for handlers who have taught a running contact, blowing a contact means the dog has launched off the equipment and failed to touch the yellow zone at all. Whatever the situation, blowing a contact is the most common reason for handler despair.

A blown contact means that the dog failed to touch the yellow zone.

If you have trained the two on/two off, your first remedial step is to go back to contact training away from the equipment. (See Chapter 11.) When your dog is solid with those exercises, return to the equipment, but keep your dog on leash so he can't make mistakes. Continue to retrain based on the assumption that he didn't really understand the expectation the first time.

If you taught your dog a running contact, try two other easy strategies. Set an 8-inch (20.3-cm) jump just 1 foot (0.3 m) or so from the base of the contact obstacle. When they see this obstacle, most dogs will run to the bottom so they can jump it. You might also try constructing a PVC arch just tall enough for the dog to run under at the bottom of the contact. Because a dog has to raise his head to jump, the arch prevents him from leaping. If these exercises are repeated frequently, the dog will be patterned to run all the way down.

If the problem persists after reteaching, it's time to move on to a new method. The following approach is based on an understanding that dogs blow off the contact because they want to keep running. What could be more fun? Your job is to short-circuit the excitement in a nonpunitive way.

Training Challenges

Here is what you can do:

1. When the dog runs off the contact without stopping (two-on/two-off) or leaps over the contact (running contact) zone, just stand still at the bottom of the obstacle.

2. Keep your arms at your side. Be silent. Your dog will notice that you are not with him and turn back to you.

3. Continue to stand still long enough for him to get the message that something is wrong. Then stand there a little longer.

4. Once you believe your message has been communicated, that something has gone awry, walk slowly back to the beginning of the obstacle. Your dog will follow you.

5. Ask him to do the obstacle again. Generally, he will get the point and do the contact as you have trained. If so, jackpot the behavior. Sometimes you may have to repeat this twice for the dog to get the idea.

6. If the dog does not get the correct behavior by the third try, put the leash back on and help him get it right.

This strategy is much tougher than it sounds. Handlers are programmed to keep moving, and standing still is a serious challenge. Have a friend videotape you to confirm that you are stopping long enough to communicate clearly with your dog.

Some handler behaviors exacerbate blown contacts or rear their head once handlers leap into competition. If your dog has good contacts and then loses them, check whether you might have slipped into one of these problematic behaviors listed on page 189.

Breaking Start Line *Stays*

Frequently, the excitement of trials causes dogs to begin releasing themselves from the start line as their handlers lead out. This is a serious problem, because you may be in a bad spot when your dog takes off. Recently, Scout the Sheltie, previously known for her rock-solid *stays*, broke and ran behind me into a tunnel in a trial before I could even lift a hand. I caught up with her, but I had already received an off-course fault, which gave me an NQ

A PVC arch patterns the dog to run to the bottom of the contact obstacle.

Blowing Contacts

Four Nasty Handler Behaviors	How to Fix Them
Handler has inconsistent criteria for the contact performance. For example, sometimes the handler allows the dog to take off from a contact without waiting for a release word	Clarify for yourself what you want your dog to do, and then stick with it. If you want your dog to wait for a release before leaving the contact, there must be a consequence, such as standing still and stopping the game when the dog blows off the obstacle. (The process for doing this is described in the previous section.)
Handler never really teaches the contact performance so that the dog understands it and can do it in a stressful situation.	Start over. Teach your dog exactly what you want. Don't trial until your dog does the contacts correctly and reliably on different equipment and in fun matches.
Handler has different expectations for the contacts in training and in trials. For example, she makes the dog hold the contacts in class but releases the dog very quickly in trials.	Align your training and trialing. If you plan to release your dog from the contact very quickly in a trial, make sure to practice that in class, along with longer periods of holding the contacts.
Handler lets the contact behavior deteriorate in trials.	Even in trials, take time periodically to reinforce the correct contact behavior with verbal praise.

(nonqualifying score) for the class.

While some training challenges occur because of the dog's personality or temperament, *stay* problems are based entirely on training issues. The chart on page 190 describes the top three things that handlers do that result in a dog who will not stay until released.

Knocking Bars

Some highly athletic and well-trained agility dogs have a single problem—they knock bars. It is a serious problem because it will result in disqualification or point deduction.

Sometimes the dog's physical structure simply makes jumping difficult. Short, long dogs and dogs with heavy

Knocking bars will result in disqualification or point deduction.

Breaking Start Line *Stays*

Three Nasty Handler Behaviors	How to Fix Them
Handler never teaches an adequate *stay* that has been proofed in high-distraction settings	Reteach an *agility stay*. Practice and reward a good *stay* at lots of fun matches and other distracting situations such as letting your other dogs race around while your competition dog has to sit still.
Handler takes off and runs a sequence in class, even if the dog has broken a *stay*.	Always stop running if your dog breaks a *stay* in practice. Say something neutral like, "Uh oh. Let's try that again." Immediately take him back to the original spot and put him back in a stay. On the flip side, remember to reward your dog regularly when he does stay in practice. The old saying, "You get what you reward" is so darn true.
Handler takes off and runs a course in a trial, even if the dog has broken a *stay*.	Stop dead still if your dog breaks. Don't look at your dog. When he returns to you, don't look at him. Stand there for an uncomfortably long time. When you know that he has gotten the point that something is wrong, go ahead and run. If this does not improve the situation on subsequent runs, try leaving the course. Don't berate your dog. Just put him away quietly. Before your next run, practice your *stay* at the practice jump, awarding lots of treats for successful stays.

front ends have to work very hard to clear jumps. For example, both Cardigan and Pembroke Welsh Corgis are notorious for knocking a single bar at the end of a spectacular run. Other dogs, however, have no such physical challenges and still knock bars.

At least a dozen reasons exist for bar knocking. If your dog shows this tendency, address it with your teacher immediately, before it becomes a habit for the dog.

The chart on page 191 addresses several common causes and strategies to fix the problem.

"Whee" Attacks

To some "green" dogs, the agility field is overly stimulating. They may perform a few obstacles and then take off and race around the course exuberantly. They may take off to visit with another dog. Sometimes observers laugh, and that, unfortunately, reinforces the behavior.

Some breeds, such as the Siberian Husky, that love to run and do not have high handler focus,

Training for Agility

Knocking Bars

Reasons Dog Knocks Bars	Training Ideas
Dog jumps flat and doesn't care that he hits the bar.	Have two training partners stand on either side of the jump and raise the bar just as he jumps. This should be high enough to clip his feet but not high enough to trip him. (This sometimes helps because it startles the dog.) Fill a hollow jump bar with sand and cap the ends. This gives it enough weight so that when the dog hits the bar, he actually feels the contact. Exclaim in surprise when your dog hits the bar, and stop him immediately. Slowly replace the bar and let him try it again. Get creative and attach a device above the jump bar that gets your dog's attention. A piece of clear fishing line can be attached to the jump stanchions using elastic so it gives if the dog hits it. (Again, this surprises the dog and sometimes encourages him to jump higher.)
Dog takes off too early, too late, or jumps inefficiently.	These problems are often the result of a dog being asked to jump too high too soon. Take the jumps back to a low height, and very gradually raise the jumps in the smallest possible increments.
Dog looks back.	Teach and use your *go on* command (Chapter 6) so that he will race down a line of jumps without turning to see where you are.
Handler talks to the dog while he is still over the jump.	Stay silent until your dog lands. Use more body language and fewer verbal commands. (This strategy is only for dogs knocking bars, not all dogs, some of whom need to hear the command while in the air.)

are notorious for engaging in "whee" attacks. However, any dog is capable of taking off. I have seen equally spectacular "whee" runs from a Papillon, a Pembroke Welsh Corgi, a Borzoi, and a Boxer.

Handlers sometimes do things to inadvertently encourage this behavior, as addressed in the chart on page 192.

Fear of the Judge

In the agility ring, the judge moves around to see your dog performing the obstacles. Some judges stand closer to the dogs than others. For dogs who are a bit shy, this can cause them to avoid an obstacle or perform it incorrectly. Scout the Sheltie was trained to ignore people in hats by having classmates bring their weirdest hat and stand around the course, including quite close to the table where her anxiety had started.

Training Challenges

"Whee" Attacks

Four Nasty Handler Behaviors	How to Fix Them
Trying to run the dog in sequences that are too long for the dog's attention span or stress level.	Divide any training runs into short sequences that the dog can handle. Stop after a set number of obstacles and reward, reward, reward. Gradually add more obstacles before you reinforce the dog for staying with you. When this training effectively short-circuits "whee" attacks in training, go to fun matches and do the same thing. Treat every obstacle, if needed, to keep your dog's attention. Gradually space the rewards out as staying with you becomes more rewarding than running wild.
Continuing to trial and hoping the behavior will disappear.	Go back to working on the training described earlier and other focus games that make being with you highly rewarding. Enter fun matches as described earlier. Don't enter trials until you have this behavior under control.
Taking a high-energy dog into the ring without an adequate release of energy.	Exercise your wild child to the point of fatigue before you go in the ring. Give him a five- or ten-minute rest after a sustained game of Frisbee or ball chasing before you go in the ring.
If your dog takes off for a run, do not call or walk toward him. This will just encourage a game.	Turn around and walk slowly out of the training area. Your dog will inevitably follow. When he finally walks up to you, put him on the leash (gently), walk him quietly to his crate, and put him in (gently).

If your dog tends to spook, enlist your friends and teacher to stand in key locations on practice courses. Start with them at a distance and move them closer as the dog relaxes.

Refusal to Sit or Down on the Table

It is surprisingly common to see dogs jump on the table and then look at their handler as if they had never heard the commands *sit* or *down*. Perhaps the table is hot for a dog with a thin coat. Perhaps the surface of the table is rough. Perhaps the dog is annoyed that he has to stop running.

If your dog has not been trained to enjoy playing on the table, as described in Chapter 13, start there. Play the table games described in that chapter regularly, even when your dog seems to have a solid table performance.

Handlers tend to demonstrate their more bizarre behaviors while their dog is on the table.

Dogs must be comfortable with the judge standing nearby.

This is undoubtedly due to anxiety that the dog won't reliably sit or down on this obstacle or won't stay down for the required five seconds. The chart on page 194 features some problems and remedies so that you can trust your dog and look like you're in control.

Running Off Course

Dogs run off course, not to be naughty, but generally because they enjoy a particular obstacle or because they simply don't know what you want. That said, some dogs try harder to figure out what you want than do others. Scout the Sheltie diligently attempts to read my directions, while Grace the Corgi is perfectly happy to blast through any nearby obstacle unless my directions are very fast and emphatic.

Dogs sometimes become infatuated with a particular obstacle. Tunnels are frequent magnets for some dogs, as we discussed before. Even the

Agility Speak

A *call-off* occurs when a dog is headed toward the "wrong" obstacle, and the handler successfully keeps the dog from performing that obstacle. In general, needing to use a call-off is a sign that the handler has not communicated clearly with the dog, but even the best handlers in the world occasionally need a call-off to keep their dog on course.

Training Challenges

Refusal to Sit or Down on the Table

Four Nasty Handler Behaviors	How to Fix Them
Bending over the dog in a body language that is intimidating.	Stand up straight.
Scowling at the dog.	Soften your expression—even smile!
Making direct eye contact.	Avert your eyes from the dog's face. Some dogs respond well if the handler rotates slightly away from them.
Training the dog to be dependent on having the handler close to hold the *sit* or *down*.	Train your dog so that you can move away toward the next obstacle. Practice moving a small step away from the table each time you train. Gradually increase the distance until your dog understands his responsibility for staying put until released.

responsible Scout has disappeared happily into many tunnels that were calling her name. The call-off training described in the chart on page 195 is now a staple in our training routine.

Stressed Dog

Handlers ask a lot of dogs in agility. Sometimes expectations get too high, and much like a person, the dog starts to show the stress. Dogs exhibit stress in a variety of ways that include racing around, sniffing, avoiding eye contact, wandering off, yawning, and slowing down. If your dog shows any of these behaviors, stop training and regroup before the joy of the game is lost.

Caution

Be careful about falling into a trap in which you blame your dog for defying you during his agility training if he doesn't do things perfectly. This mindset results in a "get tough" approach that only serves to hurt your relationship with your dog. Use any challenges during your training as an opportunity to problem-solve creatively, and make a plan to fix the issue using positive training techniques.

One story I would like to relate concerns a lovely and very fast Italian Greyhound and her handler. This young dog started training very well, but then her handler recognized how good the dog was, and she became "serious" about agility. The dog felt the pressure and stopped enjoying the game. She would wander off mid-course and start sniffing. She refused to be caught. Fortunately, the handler recognized the problem and returned to her lighthearted training. The dog returned to her previous form and has now competed at the national level.

Running Off Course

Five Nasty Handler Behaviors	How to Fix Them
Handler rewards the dog on the "harder" obstacles such as the contacts and takes the tunnel and jump performance for granted.	During training, make sure your dog is reinforced for all obstacles to avoid a preference for certain obstacles that get rewarded more frequently.
Communication with the dog using your body language is not clear.	Make sure that your feet, shoulders, and arm are pointing where you want the dog to go. Also, make sure that this communication is given in a timely fashion, so that your dog has time to react.
Limited handler moves hamper communication.	All of the handlers' moves described in Chapter 15, such as the front cross and rear cross, are powerful tools to keep your dog on course. Learn to execute these effectively to give directions to your dog.
Excessive reliance on verbal commands.	Use verbal commands only as a supplement to effective body language.
Dog is not trained to understand a call-off, particularly from a tunnel.	Practice running toward a tunnel, but use your body language and verbal command to pull your dog back to you before he runs in. This is one time it is okay to use his name. Reward him if he returns to you. Start a good distance from the tunnel at first, and get closer and closer as the dog is successful. If you can't call your dog back to you, move farther from the tunnel. Alternate with letting the dog run into the tunnel so that he doesn't start to think that the tunnel is always wrong.

Whenever you encounter a challenge in agility training, deal with it positively and creatively. If you communicate frustration to your dog, you will make the situation worse by making him nervous. Stay upbeat, and enjoy your dog!

Part 3
Competition

Chapter Eighteen

Getting Ready to Trial

O nce you have been training with your dog for some time, and you've moved past the introductory classes, your thoughts are bound to turn to competing. But where do you start?

Register Your Dog

All organizations that sanction agility trials require that your dog be registered with them before he competes in one of their trials. If you have a purebred, you are familiar with registering your dog with a kennel club. The process is similar when you register your dog for agility, whether he is a pure or mixed breed.

As soon as the thought of trialing crosses your mind, you can find the appropriate registration forms at each of the agility organization's websites listed at the end of this chapter. Each registration, which is good for the life of the dog, requires paying a small fee. In most cases, your dog must be registered before you enter a trial; allow several weeks for this process. Some organizations

Agility Speak

Historically, *registering* a dog has been limited to owners with a purebred dog. In agility, all dogs, whether a pure or mixed breed, must be registered with each sanctioning organization before you can enter their trials. The forms and fees for registration can be found on each organization's website. You will receive a registration number for your dog for each venue. Keep this in a handy place, because you will be required to provide it with each trial entry. Fun matches don't require any specific registration.

also allow you the option of joining as a member, but it is not a requirement. A personal membership provides you with specific services, such as the ability to access your dog's trial records.

Participate in Fun Matches

Fun matches, generally sponsored by regional agility clubs, are designed to serve as a transition from agility training to agility trials. They give novice handlers and experienced handlers with new dogs an opportunity to run full courses as a dress rehearsal for competing. The advantage of the fun match, other than the relaxed atmosphere, is that training is allowed in the ring. You may (and should) reward your dog with treats and toys during the run. (This is different from official trials, where toys and treats are not allowed in the ring.) Also, in a fun match, you may loop around to take a specific obstacle more than once. You may also take helpers into the ring with you. If you want to make sure that your dog doesn't get scared on a new teeter, have a friend hold the teeter as you did in training. If you want to work on your dog running ahead, recruit a pal to crouch with a treat at the end of a long line of jumps. The point is that you may use your allotted time in any way you want as long as it is positive for the dog.

Most handlers take their dogs to several fun matches before entering a competitive trial. Generally, the fun match sponsors require a minimal amount of training, such as six months, and require that the dog be able to perform the obstacles off leash. Check the fun match flyer for this information. Most agility trials have an information table with flyers about both

Fun matches are designed to serve as a transition from agility training to agility trials.

upcoming trials and fun matches. In addition, many agility teachers provide their students with information about local events that would be appropriate to enter.

You may enter your dog at any jump height at a fun match. For your first matches, it is a good idea to enter your dog at least one height below his "real" jump height. For example, Grace the Corgi recently jumped 8 inches (20.3 cm) at her first fun match, although she will compete at a 12-inch (30.5-cm) height. This strategy discourages the excited dog from going into the ring and immediately taking down jump bars, because they are asked to jump lower than the height at which they have been practicing.

Agility teachers are the best source of information about fun matches. Pre-enter if you have the option, and your runs will be scheduled earlier in the day than those who register on the day of the event.

Review the Rules

Although agility rules are similar, each agility organization has its unique twists. For example, NADAC allows training in the ring at a trial. That is, you can put a dog back on a contact obstacle if the dog makes a mistake. In other organizations, this would be a mistake resulting in automatic dismissal from the ring.

Getting Ready to Trial

Trial Measurements

Because every organization requires that dogs be measured to confirm their jump height, it is desirable to train your dog to stand nicely for this process. A wrestling match between your dog and the judge is not a good way to start a day of agility. In your classes or at fun matches, look for the two types of measuring devices you may encounter: the measuring bar and the wicket.

Practice lowering the measuring bar over your dog's shoulders and setting the wicket in the same spot. (A wicket is a PVC device that is set over a dog's back. Wickets come in different sizes, and when the wicket's "feet" touch the ground, it indicates the correct jump height.)

Each of the organizations has its rules posted on the Internet. Although you don't need to memorize the rules, it is a good idea to scan them and ask your teacher questions on any that you find unclear. Also, be aware that agility rules change regularly.

At the trial, a judge's briefing will be held before each of your runs. Judges are generally very willing to answer questions, particularly in the novice classes. Use the opportunity to ask about specific rules, but don't expect an orientation.

Attend Several Trials

Nothing is better for getting you ready to trial than spending several days at agility trials. You can get the lay of the land and see how things are done before you add the stress of competing. Contact the trial secretary to find out when the trial starts. Arrive early to observe the handler check-in and the measuring process. Walk around the different rings and observe.

If possible, take your dog so that he can get used to the sights, sounds, and smells, the other dogs, and the general hubbub of a trial. Although nonentered dogs are not encouraged at trials, in

Remember that although agility rules are similar, each agility organization has its own unique twists.

reality you will find many on the grounds. Rules apply to what type of restraints may be used—prong collars and head-type halters may not be allowed—so check the specific organization's website for that information if you plan to outfit your dog in something other than a flat collar or harness. If your dog is well behaved and correctly dressed, no one will be any the wiser for your being there with him. Just remember the etiquette: no interactions with other dogs unless you get the owner's okay. And sit back from the ring a bit so that your dog does not get overly excited and interfere with the dog who is competing.

Caution

Remember that running a course in a new location with unfamiliar equipment can be stressful for a novice dog. It is your job to make sure that your dog has a positive experience in fun matches. Plan several places that you will stop on course to praise and treat. You may want someone to hold the teeter and lower it slowly, as you did in your early training, because this is the piece of equipment most likely to make an inexperienced dog anxious.

Find competitors who are relaxing between their classes, and ask them questions. Most handlers love to share information about their sport.

Stay Healthy

You'll have more fun at your first trial if you and your dog are in good physical shape. Even though a run only lasts from 30 seconds (when you're really good and really fast) to a little more than a minute, you will be running. And depending on the trial, you'll have anywhere from two to six runs in a day. Jogging, brisk walking, and bicycling with your dog are great ways for both of you to get in shape. Be cautious about running the dog on pavement or concrete,

Make sure that your dog is in good physical shape before you enter a trial.

Getting Ready to Trial

Dog Registration Guidelines

NOTE: No agility-sanctioning body allows bitches in season, blind, lame, or aggressive dogs.

AAC
Agility Association of Canada
www.aac.ca
- Must be registered before the trial
- Must be 18 months or older
- Mixed breed and handicapped dogs welcome, as long as physically and mentally capable of performing the tests

AKC
American Kennel Club
www.akc.org
- Must be registered, either as a purebred dog or by an "Indefinite Listing Privilege" before the trial
- Must be 12 months or older
- Deaf dogs not allowed

CKC
Canadian Kennel Club
www.ckc.ca
- May enter as a "Listed Dog" and complete registration after the trial
- Must be 18 months or older
- Mixed breed dogs not allowed

CPE
Canine Performance Events, Inc.
www.k9cpe.com
- Must be registered before the trial
- Must be 15 months or older
- Mixed breed dogs allowed
- Wolves and wolf hybrids not allowed

DOCNA
Dogs on Course in North America
www.docna.com
- Must be registered before the trial
- Must be 12 months or older
- Mixed breed dogs allowed

NADAC
Northern American Dog Agility Council
www.nadac.com
- Must be registered before the trial
- Must be 18 months or older
- Mixed-breed dogs, dogs with deformities, and deaf dogs welcome

The Kennel Club
www.the-kennel-club.org.uk
- Must be registered before the trial with the Kennel Club or the Obedience and Working Trials Register
- Must be more than 18 months of age
- Mixed breeds welcome

UKA
United Kingdom Agility
www.UKAgility.com
- Must be registered with the UKA
- Must be more than 16 months of age
- Mixed breeds welcome

UKC
United Kennel Club
www.ukcdogs.com
- Must be Permanently Registered, Limited Privilege (includes mixed-breed dogs), or Temporary Listed before the trial
- Must be 6 months or older
- Deaf dogs welcome

USDAA
United States Dog Agility Association
www.usdaa.com
- Must be registered (can be registered with entry)
- Must be 18 months or older
- Mixed-breed dogs welcome
- May not have an injury or illness that would affect dog's performance
- Deaf dogs allowed

Lots of practice will help ensure that you and your dog are in top condition for agility competition.

though, because the impact can cause foot and skeletal problems.

Find yourself a good pair of shoes that will be comfortable for all-day wear and that provide adequate support for running on uneven grass. Wet, early morning grass can be quite slippery. You may want to look for shoes with soft rubber cleats marketed specifically as agility shoes. Alternatively, many people opt for light trail-running shoes.

With your dog registered, a few fun matches under your belt, and the agility rules studied, you are on the path toward your first trial. Your next step is to begin assembling the equipment and supplies that you will need to stay comfortable during the weekends that you spend at agility events.

Getting Ready to Trial

Chapter Nineteen

Packing
It Up

Because you will spend long (and wonderful) days at agility trials, it is important to assemble the resources you and your dog will need to be comfortable. It is also useful to establish a routine for assembling your agility supplies so that you spend minimal time getting ready to go. You will know you are serious about the sport when you simply keep your van, truck, or SUV loaded from weekend to weekend.

Essential Big Items

Let's take a look at the big stuff that will contribute to your comfort over an agility weekend. I can't imagine leaving any of these items at home!

Your Dog

I once knew a Texan who made it 200 miles from home before he remembered that he had not loaded his dog. This may be a single event in the history of agility. Nonetheless, it is good to do a head count before pulling out of the driveway.

Agility Speak

The *exercise pen*, or *ex pen*, is the most useful dog item ever invented, or so it sometimes seems. The ex pen consists of eight sides that fold like a fan. When closed, it is easy to carry and pack. Once open, it makes a spacious area for one or more dogs to stretch out and sleep. At agility trials, you will see many agility pens housing several dog friends who are napping and playing with toys or each other. An ex pen definitely becomes a dog's home away from home.

Crates

Traveling safely in the car requires containment of some sort for your dog. In the car, the safest crate is the plastic variety that is approved for airline travel. The crate should be tightly strapped down to avoid having it roll in the case of an accident. However, on a hot day, a plastic crate becomes a sauna, so either a wire crate, a soft mesh crate, or an exercise pen is better at the trial.

Exercise Pens

The majority of dogs are most comfortable in an exercise pen at a trial. Besides, the exercise pen is easy to fold up and transport. If your dog is likely to try to jump out, commercial canvas tops are available that eliminate this escape route. In any case, trying out a new method of containment on a trial day is not a good idea. Recently, I watched a hoard of people in pursuit of a Rottweiler who had been left in a new mesh crate. She was making remarkably good time traveling across the show grounds like a hamster in a plastic ball.

Tents

Most people purchase a canopy. Size preferences vary, but the average size seems to get bigger each year. The average size is 10 feet (3.0 m) by 10 feet (3.0 m), although some people even go one size larger. Some tents are larger than the first house I purchased and are definitely more comfortable. A few people try to get by with a beach-type umbrella that they rotate throughout the day to keep themselves and their dog in a tiny patch of shade.

Tent Floors

Our dogs cannot, of course, be on the *grass*. One must have a floor cover. For this purpose, most people use inexpensive plastic mats that can be easily scrubbed when you get home.

The majority of dogs are most comfortable in an exercise pen at a trial.

Competition

Tent Walls

To maximize shade, some sort of shade cloth is required. Originally, people used garden shade cloth, attaching it with large metal clips, but in recent years, tent walls have become highly sophisticated and expensive. The best ones not only block the sun but also allow air to circulate so that heat does not build up inside the tent. This high-tech material could be worn by an astronaut in a pinch.

Some dogs prefer the exercise pen, and others are comfortable in a soft crate.

Dog Beds

Dogs need soft beds for hours of lounging. Some handlers bring simple pads, and others opt for elaborate beds.

Chairs

Because agility trials take many hours, comfortable seating is essential for handlers, too. Luxurious canvas chairs have replaced the basic lawn chair, and many of them feature cup holders and headrests. A few people even toss in lounge chairs for a quick catnap.

Ice Chests

Dog treats, human treats, cold water, electrolyte drinks, crackers, salami, granola bars—you name it, handlers bring it.

Friends

Hauling this stuff from the car to the trial site and back to the car alone is painful. There has never been a better

Caution

Agility competitors hit the road very early to make it to the show on time. Trials often go until late into the afternoon, and plenty of excitement can wear you out. Getting sleepy while driving home is a very real danger. Make sure to make a plan regarding what you will do to stay awake. If you get too tired, just pull over and take a catnap. (Dare I say that after a dog show?)

Packing It Up

reason to make travel friends, even if it means getting up a half-hour early to rendezvous.

Extreme Gear

More and more specialized items are showing up in the agility tenting area. It is not unusual to see small pools for dog wetting and foot soaking, tents with misting hoses, or a full-sized picnic table that folds to the size of a shoebox.

A typical trial setup includes canopy, sides, and floor mat.

I am a minimalist compared to many other competitors. I still make do with a spray bottle on hot days, while my neighbor's tent resembles a cool day in the rain forest as the steady stream of droplets reduces the heat inside by a good 20 degrees. I notice that those of us in the spray bottle crowd seem to find reasons to drop in and chat with our cool neighbors around 2:00 on a scorching afternoon.

Dressing for Agility

Dressing for agility deserves a special note. Chilly early morning arrivals and toasty afternoons require good layering that can be gradually removed. I have often been happy that I tossed in an extra jacket, a pair of long pants, or a pair of shorts. Last, if I could take only one extra item, it would be a pair of dry socks for the drive home. These come in handy after many hours of soaked feet from trotting around on wet grass.

Small Items

Then there are bags of all the regular stuff, such as leashes, poop bags, confirmation forms, dog first-aid kit (including antihistamines in case of a bee sting), wallet, and all the other stuff we can't bear to be without. All the small items you will need are listed below.

I find it useful to sort these things into separate bags: dog comfort, human comfort, shelter comfort, print materials for the trial, and motel items. You will undoubtedly find your own system, but this is what works well for me.

Competition

Dog Comfort

- Crate
- Exercise pen
- Dog bed
- Leash
- Dog bowls
- Water
- Poop pick-up bags
- Toys and chews
- Treats
- Collar with no tags or a slip lead
- Dog first-aid kit
- Towels for drying wet pups
- Your vet's phone number

Human Comfort

- Clothes, shoes (including extra pair of shoes and socks), and toiletries if staying overnight
- Sunscreen
- Rain gear
- Meals, drinks, and snacks
- Ice chest
- Folding chair
- Emergency phone number
- Something to keep you awake and give you energy on the drive home, such as books on tape, several containers of coffee, and/or sunflower seeds

Shelter Comfort

- Canopy, tent, or umbrella
- Tent walls
- Tarp ground cover
- Bungee cords or clips to fasten sides

Print Materials for the Trial

- Confirmation/premium
- Directions/map
- Jump height card
- Rules from the sponsoring organization
- Pen or pencil
- Trial log or notebook to record your results

Motel Items

- Directions/map from trial to motel
- Motel confirmation
- Sheets (to protect the motel bedspread)
- Dog's regular food
- Alarm clock

Once you have assembled all your accoutrements, you are ready to start your competitive agility career. Let's get going to that first trial.

Chapter Twenty

Your First Trial

The time you dreamed of and worked toward has arrived. Your dog is running long sequences on the agility course with confidence. You have entered several fun matches, and your dog performed the obstacles safely, responded to your commands, and played the game with enthusiasm. It may be time to take the leap and enter a real trial. In this chapter, I'll share the ropes with you, from deciding whether or not to compete to walking out of the ring after your first trial run.

Double-Check That Your Dog Is Ready

This first step is most important. Make absolutely sure your dog is ready. A surprising number of people enter a trial before their dog really knows how to weave, for instance. I recommend that your dog "clear the bar" on the following five criteria:

1. Your teacher says you are ready.
2. Your dog knows how to perform all the obstacles.
3. He has a rock-solid *sit/stay* at the start line.

4. He comes when called, both in and out of the ring.

5. He focuses on you no matter how distracting the environment.

If the answer is muddy for any of these points, don't enter yet. Continue with your classes. You have a whole agility career ahead of you, and it makes a lot more sense to go into the ring with a fully trained dog than with a partially trained dog who might get scared or develop bad habits.

Locate Trials

When the answer is yes to the criteria listed above, it's time to locate agility trials close to home. I am assuming that you have registered your dog with the agility organizations as recommended in Chapter 18. If not, do that immediately, because the process may take several weeks.

You can locate trials in several ways:

■ Initially, you can find trials listed on the websites of the agility-sponsoring organizations (see Chapter 18), with links to the entry forms, called *premiums*.

One measure of your dog's readiness to compete in formal competition is whether he is able to focus on you, no matter how distracting the environment.

Competition

Download, print, and fill out the entry form.

- Many websites provide calendars of trials by region. Talk with your agility teacher to find an address for your area.
- When you visit agility trials, you will find an information table; generally, you will find premiums for upcoming trials in your area.
- Once you have entered trials, you will begin to receive e-mail notices of upcoming trials. A single keystroke connects you with the information you need to enter.

In densely populated areas, it is possible to trial several times a month. Before long, you will find yourself making decisions about how many trials you have the time and resources to enter.

Fill Out the Premium

When you have your premium in hand for a particular trial, start by checking out the opening date and the deadline for the show secretary to receive the entry. Some trials accept entries any time after the forms are published, but many have an opening date for postmarks and will not accept earlier entries. Some trials fill up on the opening date, so it's always a good idea to mail your entry as early as allowed.

Agility Speak

An agility *premium*, besides containing the entry form for your dog, will include other important information, such as motels near the show site that accept dogs, camping options, emergency veterinary care, directions to the show, and whom to contact if you have questions. It is a good idea to put your premium in your travel kit after you have sent in your entry.

Initially, you may find the premiums a bit confusing. You must include:

- Your choice of class. For example, in the AKC you select between Standard or Preferred classes. In USDAA, you opt for Championship or Performance classes In each case, the latter offers lower jump heights. You might choose to put an older dog in a Veteran's class or a young handler in the Junior's class.
- Your dog's height. Enter your best estimate, even though it may change during your official measurement at the trial. (See Chapter 9.)
- Your dog's jump height. (See details on next page.)
- The specific events that you want to enter. Sometimes, handlers start dogs in Novice Jumpers classes, which are less complex than the Novice Standard classes, in order to get the dog oriented to the trial environment. Others take the big leap and enter all the games.

- Your dog's registration information. (See Chapter 18.)

With the entry form, you will also find a volunteer form to work. Some of the jobs at a trial are pretty easy, whereas others, such as timer or scribe, are more technical and can be intimidating at first. The volunteer form will allow you to check off the jobs that you feel comfortable performing. Clubs often encourage volunteer workers by providing free lunches and a workers-only raffle.

A week or so before the trial, you will receive confirmation from the club that your entry was received. Generally, this form includes the numbers of dogs in each class and other key information, such as the order of the classes, the process for measuring dogs, and the time of the first course walk-through. Some confirmation envelopes include the numbers you should wear while running. Make sure to tuck these items into the supplies you pack.

Indicate Your Jump Height

Each premium will ask what height your dog will jump. By now, you have measured your dog as closely as possible. With that information in hand, go to the website of the organization sponsoring the trial and search for "jump heights." Since each organization has different cut-off points for jump heights, make sure to check each time you try a different venue.

Let's look at AKC rules as our sample case. Here is what you will find for the Standard classes:

- 8-inch (20.3-cm) jump height for dogs 10 inches (25.4 cm) and under at the withers
- 12-inch (30.5-cm) jump height for dogs 14 inches (35.6 cm) and under at the withers
- 16-inch (40.6-cm) jump height for dogs 18 inches (45.7 cm) and under at the withers
- 20-inch (50.8-cm) jump height for dogs 22 inches (55.9 cm) and under at the withers
- 24-inch (61.0-cm) jump height for dogs over 22 inches (55.9 cm) at the withers

If these heights sound too challenging for your dog, another option is available. In the Preferred class, dogs jump one level lower than in Standard. For example, dogs over 22 inches (55.9 cm) at the withers jump at 20 inches (50.8 cm), and dogs who jump 20 inches (50.8 cm) in Standard jump 16 inches (40.6 cm) in Preferred.

Once you have this information, circle the correct jump height on the premium. If your dog is close to a cut-off, always indicate the lower height. This is very important, because when your dog is measured on trial day, the judge can move your dog to a higher jump height, but she cannot move him to a lower height.

Secure Reservations

As soon as you mail your entry, consider accommodations if the trial is at a distance from your home. Most trials start by 8:00 a.m. Remember that you may need to get up early for trials, and driving back and forth fatigued can be dangerous. I have a two-hour rule—less than two hours one way, I commute; more than two hours, I stay over. If you have an RV, trailer, or tent, camping areas often are available near the agility trial grounds.

Set Up

When you arrive at the trial, locate a good area for your canopy or shelter. See the previous chapter for more details about packing and setting up at the trial.

A premium will ask what height your dog will jump.

Check In and Get Measured

After setting up, find the check-in table. Ask the people working at the check-in table when and where the judge will be measuring. Often, you will be asked to complete your measurement before you pick up the schedule and running order for each ring, the maps for each course, and your numbers (if the organization uses them).

Check the Work Schedule

If you signed up to work, check the work assignment sheets. Some trial organizers provide a sheet that shows worker assignments for all the rings, and some provide a separate list for each ring.

Your First Trial

Review the Trial Schedule

By looking at the schedule, you can see the order of classes in each ring for the entire trial. Novice classes sometimes run later in the day, but not always.

If you follow another class in a ring, it is possible to estimate, very roughly, when you should be watching for your first class. Let's imagine that your Starters Jumpers class follows an Advanced Jumpers class of 60 dogs. Running the first class will take at least an hour at a minute per dog. Then, resetting the obstacles for your Novice class will take at least 15 minutes.

At some trials, the Standard course is run first. At other trials, the Jumpers class or another game such as Pairs or Gamblers might be run right off the bat.

Memorize Your First Course

Use your free time to memorize the course for whatever class you have first. If you memorize the course before you walk it, you will be ahead of the learning curve. After you complete your first run, memorize your second course. Later in your agility career, you will memorize multiple courses simultaneously, but this is an advanced skill.

During the walk-through, handlers memorize the course and plan how they are going to handle it.

218

Walk Your Course

As courses are being set for a particular class, you will notice that competitors begin to gather around the ring to watch. Many have their maps in hand. They are comparing the map to the actual course.

As soon as all the obstacles are in place according to the judge's plan, the ring steward or judge will announce that the ring is open for walk-through. Your time for walking, determined by the ring judge, is generally around 15 minutes, but it varies widely. The walk-through is the time to make sure you know where to go on course, to solidify your understanding of the course's challenges, and to plan specifically what you will do to handle it.

Memorizing your course prior to your run will help you and your dog succeed in competition.

These are a few questions to ask yourself:

- Should I lead out from the start line?
- Realistically, how far can I lead out without my dog breaking his stay?
- Are there any places where he will need extra help to see the correct obstacle?
- Should I front or rear cross anywhere on the course?
- What areas are particularly tricky? How will I handle them?
- Are there places I anticipate needing to use my dog's name to get his attention?
- Where is the finish line that stops the watch?

Frequently, the walk-through is divided by jump heights to avoid overcrowding. An announcement is made at the ring. When the walk-through is split, handlers of small dogs—generally 8- (20.3-cm) to 16-inch (40.6-cm) dogs—walk together and then complete their runs. Then, handlers of big dogs walk through as a group and run. On the next day, the big dogs might walk and run first. This system is designed to keep handlers from having to remember the course for long periods of time and to cut down on congestion during the walk-through.

Your First Trial

Attend Your Briefing

At some point in your walk-through, the judge will call for a briefing. The expectation is that all handlers will stop walking and gather to get an overview of the course. During the briefing, the judge will generally review essential rules, such as the Four-Paw Rule, and any unique challenges on a course; she will then announce the course times and answer questions. The judge will also tell the class when each dog should enter the ring. The standard procedure is that the next dog approaches the starting line when the previous dog is on the final third of the course.

Check Your Dog Into Classes

Although you checked your dog into the trial when you arrived, you must check your dog in again for each class in which you are entered. At the entrance to each ring, you will find an easel with a list of dogs in the class. The list is usually set up during your walk-through. When the end of your walk is announced, make sure to stop by the easel and put a check by your dog's name to tell the gate steward, the person in charge of getting each team into the ring in a timely fashion, that you are present.

The ringside check-in sheet is very useful for telling you how long it will be until you run. By counting the number of dogs before your turn, you can estimate how much time you have left to prepare for your run.

Agility Speak

The *Four-Paw Rule* states that if a dog gets four paws on any of the contact obstacles and then jumps off before completing it, he may not try it again during that run. If the handler puts the dog back on, the judge stops the team and does not allow them to finish the course. This is a safety rule to prevent the handler from pressuring a dog to complete an obstacle for which he is not ready.

Prepare Your Dog

During the day, I walk my dogs every couple of hours. These are casual rambles to potty and take a look at the rings. Then, about 20 minutes before run time, I take out the dog who is going to compete. We potty one more time and then begin our warm-up routine. As with any athlete, it is good to have a regular routine.

Our routine has a number of steps. First, I replace her collar and leash with a slip lead. Not only does that prevent me from leaving the collar on in a venue that does not allow collars, but it tells my dog that we are getting ready to go. We then go for a slow jog

Maintain your connection to your dog by playing a game while you are waiting to run.

for two or three minutes. I don't allow her to sniff or visit during this time. When we are both warm, I bring out the favorite toy at a distance from the ring guaranteed not to distract a dog who might be competing. For Scout the Sheltie, this is a canvas Frisbee, and Grace the Corgi loves her food bag. I throw the toy several times and play tug to build excitement, and then we practice commands such as *turn* and *down* with toy or food reinforcement to get connected.

Next, we go to the warm-up jump that is provided near each ring, and I ask my dog to jump several times. At the warm-up jump, I practice any moves that will help me on the course, such as a long lead out or tight front cross. During this routine, I reinforce the dog's behavior with treats, but I am careful to take any food or food bag out of my pocket before I enter the ring.

The only time this routine changes is if we are scheduled to be the first team in the ring. In that case, I do the warm-up as described and then put my dog back in her pen while I walk the course. During the briefing, I ask the judge how long it will be until she wants the first dog on the start line. As soon as necessary, I walk to the tent to get my dog and jog with her back to the ring. If there is time, I do a couple of warm-up jumps.

Your First Trial

Stash Your Treats and Toys

When your run is over, you will want to give your dog positive reinforcement immediately for doing his best job—even if it was not perfect. To do this, you need to find a place at a legal distance from the ring exit where you can store your food bag or toy. Ask a friend to hold the treats, or put them on your chair.

I try not to let a novice dog see me drop the food stash. Occasionally, a young dog will take off out of the ring to go right to the rewards. As your dog becomes more experienced, this will cease to be a problem.

Final Preparation

Make sure that you and your dog are near the gate to the ring five or six dogs before your turn. At most rings, a canopy is erected to keep your dog out of the sun. Gate stewards and judges put a high priority on running rings efficiently, because hundreds of runs a day will be held. Check out the gate steward's list of dogs to see what dog is ahead of yours.

These final minutes before running are very important. Many handlers who are nervous ignore their dogs as they watch others run. The dog begins to sniff or interact with other dogs, and the connection between handler and dog dissipates. You can maintain your focus and your connection to your dog by having a game that you play with your dog at this critical time. Many handlers use their tug game to keep their dog ready to go. One Jack Russell handler I see at trials has a game in which her dog touches her hand with her nose to earn treats.

When the dog ahead of you reaches the obstacle the judge has designated, move your dog to the start line. Hold your dog, but strip him down as much as possible. For example, I remove my dog's leash but hold it around her neck so there is no danger of her chasing the dog on course. Make sure your dog is behind the start line. Nervous novices sometimes inch over the line. Look to the timer (not the judge) to tell you when to go.

> ### Collars and Leashes
>
> Some agility organizations allow dogs to wear their collars in the ring as long as they have no tags that might catch on an obstacle. Other organizations do not allow collars, and a dog is automatically disqualified if he runs with it on. The safest strategy is to remove your dog's collar and use a slip lead that is easy to remove before the run and put on after the run.

Competition

Run the Course

When the timer says you are cleared to go, the game is on. Run the course the way you walked it. Remember, even in this charged setting, the point is to have fun with your dog.

If by chance your dog makes a mistake on a contact obstacle, remember that in most agility venues, you must go on. On the other hand, if your dog makes a mistake on noncontact obstacles, such as going in the wrong end of a tunnel or missing the entry of the weave poles, you can go back and fix it. Most novice classes allow you to make several mistakes and still qualify as long as you complete all the obstacles in order, even with a detour or two.

Completing Your Run

As soon as your dog crosses the finish line, which stops your time, call him back to you and put his leash on. Some judges will specifically ask handlers to leash their dog before leaving the ring. If your dog races out of the ring without being under control, a judge may disqualify you.

Celebrate With Your Dog

Agility may seem serious to you, but for your dog, it is just a fun game to play with you. Dogs are immensely sensitive to your expressions, body language, and words. It is terribly important that, even if you are disappointed with a run, you do not communicate that emotion to your dog. I have watched many handlers take the edge off their dogs' enthusiasm for the sport by leaving the ring and stopping to chat before rewarding their dogs or by sounding disappointed.

When you finish your run, use your happiest voice with your dog as you put on his leash, which will be left for you at the finish line by a leash runner. Run directly to the treats or toy that you left near the ring. Deliver a jackpot, or play a fast and furious game that your dog enjoys.

This dog qualified (green ribbons) and placed four times (blue ribbons) at this trial.

Caution

Don't be in a rush to enter competition trials. Too many handlers enter shows before their dogs really know how to perform all the obstacles in a new, exciting setting. The result is that the dog gets anxious or practices an undesirable behavior, such as blasting by the weave pole entry or leaping off the contact. Many people say that they are entering to see how their dog will do. It is better to enter when you *know* how your dog will do.

Cool Your Dog

As with any athlete, your dog should be methodically cooled down. A slow walk for about five minutes will help his muscles to clear the waste products resulting from exercise and minimize the chances of stiffness. I like to walk my dog a bit. Then, she gets a small drink, walks some more, drinks, and so on until she isn't thirsty anymore. Then I put her back in the pen for a good nap before the next run.

Evaluate Your Performance

While you are running your dog, the judge uses a variety of hand signals to communicate any mistakes you make to a scribe sitting in the ring. A volunteer worker is timing your run from start to finish line, using a stop watch or electronic timer. As soon as you finish your run, your time is added to your scribe sheet, which is then delivered to the score table.

At the table, the workers determine if you have qualified or not, based on your point deductions and running time. In all agility venues, novice teams are allowed more deductions and time to run a course than are advanced teams.

Individual team scores are then transferred to a class sheet that indicates whether each team qualified or didn't qualify. In some cases, but not all, the team's course time is included. The sheets also indicate whether a team placed from first to fourth, based on deductions and time.

These sheets are posted with varying degrees of efficiency. When they are hung, check them out to see how you did. Ask the workers at the score table if you have questions. They are able to refer to your scribe sheet to see what the judge scored.

Competition

On the score sheets, you will find several results. You may *qualify (Q)*, which means that you met the criteria of this class both in terms of performing the obstacles and satisfying the time it took to complete the course. On the other hand, you may have a run that is *nonqualifying (NQ)*. This means that your dog did not perform all of the obstacles, blew a contact, knocked a bar, or took too much time. You may also have received an NQ if something went seriously wrong, such as breaking the Four-Paw Rule, carrying food or a toy on course, or in the judge's opinion, disciplining the dog too harshly.

Earning Titles

Dogs earn agility titles in each organization and each class by accumulating the requisite number of Qs. For example, three Qs in Starters Standard in USDAA earn a dog the SSA (Starters Standard Agility) title. Three Qs in AKC Jumpers earn a dog the NAJ (Novice Agility Jumpers) title. Among the major agility organizations, virtually dozens of titles are accessible to your dog. You need not worry that they might run out of new titles, no matter how long you and your canine partner compete.

Most agility titles are listed after a dog's name, such as Joy's Girl Scout AX MXJ AD AJ CL3. The agility organizations will send you a certificate for each title that you earn. Set aside a wall in your house for framing these handsome documents.

Keep track of each Q as you earn it. When you first qualify, you think you will never forget, but if you continue to compete in several organizations, it is very easy to lose track of what titles your dog has completed and how many legs he has earned toward the next title. Agility record books are available for this purpose.

Chapter Twenty-One

Minding Your Agility Manners

Virtually every culture has a set of rules about behavior—an etiquette that defines what is acceptable and what is not. Agility is no different. Guidelines help keep agility events running smoothly and relationships positive. In this chapter, I'll share the top 15 unwritten rules that will help you seamlessly enter the world of agility. A number of these rules have been mentioned in previous chapters, but they are all worth repeating.

#1: Set Up With Consideration

When you arrive at a trial, setting up your tent and accoutrements is the first chore. Deciding where to set up deserves some thought. If you have yappy dogs or dogs who lunge at other pups who come nearby, do not set up in an area with a lot of foot traffic. Find a quiet, distant corner of the tenting area, and save everyone at the trial (including your dogs) much annoyance. In addition, you can sometimes minimize these behaviors by screening the dog's pen so that he can't see all the activity. A few beach towels clipped onto the exercise pen provide

Make sure to keep food and toys away from the ring.

a simple, low-tech way to block the dog's view.

#2: Pay Attention to Parking

Pay attention to the trial's parking rules. If the premium says, "You can drive in to drop off your equipment, but then you must move your vehicle to the parking lot," do it. Trials are sometimes delayed because handlers must be tracked down to move their cars.

#3: Supervise Dog Interactions

Although most agility dogs are fine with other dogs, the rules of agility etiquette dictate that dogs be limited from interacting with other dogs unless the other dog's handler gives permission. A high possibility of dog-to-dog contact occurs while you are waiting in the measuring line, hanging out in the on-deck area prior to running, and walking around in the tenting area.

#4: Share the Practice Jump

At each trial, practice jumps are provided for warming up the dogs. When space allows, a jump is provided for each ring. If several dogs want to jump, the dog whose turn is coming up the soonest has priority. Even if it is your turn, however, be careful not to camp at the jump. Jump as many times as your dog needs to get ready, and then get out of the way for the next dog.

#5: Arrive at Your Ring Promptly

Agility trials are lengthy events. They move along much more smoothly when competitors check in at the gate and get in the on-deck area about five dogs ahead. Most gate stewards appreciate it if you tell them that your dog is in the area.

Agility Speak

The *on-deck* area is the area just outside the entry to a competition ring at an agility trial. Dogs and handlers who will be running soon assemble there to expedite each team getting into the ring quickly. In general, a tent shades the on-deck area for outdoor trials. Let the ring steward know you are there, because it is her job to keep the ring moving quickly.

#6: Limit the Use of the On-Deck Area

On warm days, most clubs provide a large tent at outside trials to shade the area where dogs are waiting to run. As the temperature climbs, this shaded spot becomes very popular with both agility teams and sweaty spectators. While certainly understandable, it means that the dogs whose turn to run is coming up fast can't squeeze in. Etiquette says that when you aren't preparing to run, find another place to hunker down out of the sun.

#7: Pick up After Your Dogs

Agility trial organizers are required to leave the grounds clean when the event is over. Do your part: Pack your pockets with pick-up bags, and use them with your dog, even if you are walking on the fringes of the trial area. If by chance you get caught empty-handed, ask people nearby if they have a bag. Most dog owners are happy to share.

#8: Use the Proper Leash for the Situation

If you are headed to the outback for a potty run, flexible leashes are fine. If you are in a congested area near the rings or trial table, though, use a regular lead to control your pup. This avoids big tangles and keeps interactions between excited dogs under control.

#9: Keep Food and Toys Away From the Ring

Make sure to keep your food and toys away from the ring. This includes cleaning out your pockets when headed onto the course. If you have a dog who needs to exercise, play a long distance from the rings so that it does not tempt the dogs who are competing to join you (assuming that the trial allows loose dogs at all).

#10: Be Kind to Trial Workers

Trials are run largely by volunteers. Agility club members and handlers like you work hard to keep every aspect of the event running. Should there be a moment when you are frustrated by something, resist the urge to speak harshly to anyone. Problems really can get resolved without outbursts.

#11: Never Tie Your Dog

Occasionally, competitors tether dogs to water faucets, table legs, and tent poles while they walk the course or attend to personal hygiene. This is dangerous for the dog and dangerous for dogs walking by. If you get caught in a situation where you need to do something away from your dog, ask someone to hold him *briefly*.

#12: Applaud Performances

Agility is distinguished from other sports by the support competitors give each other. One of the ways to show support as a spectator is to applaud each run. Stating the obvious, some runs are better than others, but every run reflects extensive training and certainly an element of risk-taking on the part of the handler. Resist the urge to talk about others unless your comments are positive.

Applauding another competitor's run is a great way to promote good sportsmanship.

230

#13: Volunteer to Work

Every class has chores that must be completed, from the truly mindless to the more complex. As mentioned previously, in your trial entry a work sign-up sheet will be included. If by chance you forgot to send it in, find the work crew coordinator at the trial and volunteer your services.

#14: Don't Tell People What They Did Wrong (Unless They Ask)

It is always easier to see from the sidelines what has gone wrong with a run. "Ooh," you think from the comfort of your lawn chair, "look at her arm pointing at the wrong end of the tunnel." Nothing is wrong with this observation—we learn from watching others. Agility etiquette dictates that we keep these thoughts to ourselves, however, unless a handler asks us directly to critique her run. This rule is broken most frequently between friends. The bottom line is that, if you want to make or stay friends, keep your comments positive.

> **Caution**
>
> Choose your words carefully when you talk to others about their run. It is easy to bruise a friend's feeling with a seemingly innocent comment. There is always something positive to say, even about a run that is not perfect. For example, you might say, "What a great start line stay," "That was a terrific front cross," or "You and your dog looked like you were having so much fun together."

#15: Limit the Details About Your Run

Each of our runs in agility is immensely interesting to us; however, when other handlers ask how you did, they usually do not want to know what happened obstacle by obstacle. Keep your answer short and sweet.

Agility is a big world, but you will move in an agility community that is local. You will see the same faces at agility classes and become remarkably familiar with nearby competitors when you begin to trial. If you follow the 15 rules outlined in this chapter, you are guaranteed to make and keep your new friends.

Afterword

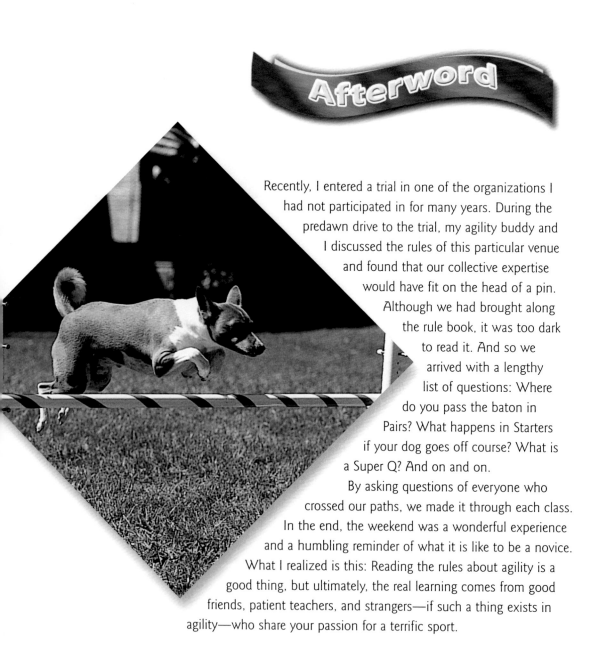

Recently, I entered a trial in one of the organizations I had not participated in for many years. During the predawn drive to the trial, my agility buddy and I discussed the rules of this particular venue and found that our collective expertise would have fit on the head of a pin. Although we had brought along the rule book, it was too dark to read it. And so we arrived with a lengthy list of questions: Where do you pass the baton in Pairs? What happens in Starters if your dog goes off course? What is a Super Q? And on and on.

By asking questions of everyone who crossed our paths, we made it through each class. In the end, the weekend was a wonderful experience and a humbling reminder of what it is like to be a novice. What I realized is this: Reading the rules about agility is a good thing, but ultimately, the real learning comes from good friends, patient teachers, and strangers—if such a thing exists in agility—who share your passion for a terrific sport.

I hope that my love for agility has come through in these pages. As I wrote long ago in Chapter 1, if you decide to participate in agility, you are embarking on a wonderful adventure with your dog. Here are the last few ideas I would like to leave with you:

■ No matter how he does in agility training or competition, be kind to your dog. He just wants to play with you.

■ Agility may become important to you, but remember, it is just a game. Keep it simple, and have fun.

■ Support the camaraderie that distinguishes the agility culture by remaining positive in all your interactions with others.

■ Go ahead and sell the house to get that place with a flat acre for your dog and agility equipment.

I look forward to meeting you on the agility field.

Build Your Own Agility Equipment

Your progress in agility will increase dramatically if you and your dog can practice and build your skills for a few minutes each day. With a little space in your backyard or at a nearby park, you can make a few of the basic agility obstacles go a long way. Using as few as three jumps, you can work a number of sequencing drills, practice rear and front crosses, directional cues, distance work, and lead outs. Throw in a different obstacle, and obstacle discrimination drills become possible.

A growing cottage industry of "backyard builders" offers relatively inexpensive agility equipment constructed from PVC pipe and lumber. Check locally with agility and dog training clubs, or check Internet resources under "agility equipment." While most inexpensive equipment might not be suitable for competition, it is sturdy enough for home use.

For those of you who are comfortable with small-scale construction projects, building your own customized obstacles can be fun and save money. The following plans for simple equipment use readily available and inexpensive materials. Use the plans to get you started and to give you ideas as you invent your own equipment. Keep in mind, however, your own safety as you construct, and your dog's safety in using the finished product. Be sure to use protective clothing, gloves, and eyewear as you work with tools, glues, and solvents. Use clamps appropriately to hold parts of your project as you work. Always check your design and finished product to make sure no protruding sharp edges or projectiles could injure you or your dog during training.

Building Jumps

Simple bar jumps are usually constructed to fit jump bars with a width of 48 inches (121.9 cm) and standards (sides) 36 inches (91.4 cm) high. (See Figure 1.)

Figure 1

Tools

- Hacksaw or PVC pipe cutter
- Clamps and worktable
- Vice grips
- Tape measure
- Marker

Materials

- 3 10-foot (3.0 m) lengths of ¾-inch schedule 40 PVC pipe
- 6 ¾-inch (1.9 cm) PVC end caps
- 4 ¾-inch (1.9 cm) PVC tees
- 4 ¾-inch (1.9 cm) snap-on jump cups (or see making Jump Cups, next section)
- PVC cement
- Vinyl tape (color of your choice)

Building Instructions

1. Measure and mark the lengths shown on the PVC pipe. Cut pipe with hacksaw and vice grip or PVC cutter:
2. Clean and de-burr the PVC cut edges with a piece of medium-grit sandpaper.
3. Assemble and glue together each side of the jump. It is a good idea to first assemble the jump without glue to ensure the correct fit. Once you are happy with the fit, take the jump apart in manageable sections to secure with PVC glue. Work on a flat surface to ensure the vertical and horizontal pieces are glued at the correct angles.

   3a. Use two tees and a 2-inch (5.1-cm) length of pipe to create a modified 4-way cross. Connect the tees such that one tee will lie flat on the ground, and the other tee will

#	Length
2	48 in (121.9 cm)
2	36 in (91.4 cm)
1	49 in (124.5 cm)
4	10 in (25.4 cm)
2	2 in (5.1 cm)

connect to hold the vertical standard and the horizontal cross bar. Make sure the connected tees are glued to form right angles. (See Figures 2 and 3.)

3b. Insert two 10-inch (25.4-cm) lengths of pipe at the opposite ends of each tee to create the base for each side, which will lie flat on the ground.

3c. Insert the 36-inch (91.4-cm) vertical standards in the tee cross opening on each side.

3d. Glue end caps on each of the 10-inch (25.4-cm) pipe ends and on each of the 36-inch (91.4-cm) vertical standards.

4. Connect each side of the jump together using the 49-inch (124.5-cm) bar, without using glue. Check the fit of the jump bars on the jump cups and make adjustments to the 49-inch (124.5-cm) bar to ensure proper fit.

5. Measure and mark the jump heights you want to set for your bars on each side of the jump.

6. Attach the jump cups so that the top of the bar in the cup aligns with the height you marked. If you are using snap-on cups, adjust the cup and bar up or down to align. If you are making (or buying) permanent cups to attach, one way to ensure correct placement height of the cup is to cut a short (2-inch [5.1-cm]) length of pipe from your excess stock. Holding the 2-inch (5.1-cm) length of pipe in the cup with one hand, align the top of the pipe length with the jump height mark while you mark the standard to align with the bottom of the cup. Use the cup mark to permanently attach the jump cup.

7. Set the jump bars in the cups. The bars should be easily knocked out of the cups. If the bars are too tight, trim a bit of length from each bar; if too loose, cut a little from the 49-inch (124.5-cm) bar that connects the standards. Work in small increments until you have the correct fit.

8. Use colored vinyl tape to create a contrasting color for easy visibility.

If you will be transporting your equipment often, leave enough parts unglued so that the jump can be easily disassembled to fit your vehicle.

Figure 2

The Beginner's Guide to Dog Agility

Making Jump Cups

Unless you love fiddling around with tools and PVC, it is far easier to buy jump cups than it is to make them. A wide variety of jump cups are available for purchase at prices cheaper than homemade (assuming you factor in your time and labor). Many designs for jump cups are possible; the following plan makes one adjustable snap-on cup from one PVC tee. (See Figure 4.)

Figure 3

Materials
- 1-inch (2.54-cm) schedule-40 PVC tee
- PVC cement

Tools
- Hacksaw
- Clamps and worktable

Building Instructions
1. Clamp the tee firmly, so that you can cut off one end of the tee, leaving an L-shaped piece.
2. Clamp again so that you can cut away the front top half of the tee opening on the now L-shaped piece, leaving a cup to support the bar.
3. Clamp each L-shaped piece so that you can cut slightly less than half of the back away, creating an expansion slot in the back.

Figure 4

Constructing a Table

The table obstacle is normally 36-inches (91.4-cm) square and varies in height from 8 inches (20.3 cm) to 24 inches (61.0 cm), depending on the height of your dog and the specifications of the agility organization. A simple plywood top placed on cement blocks or bricks can make an improvised table to use for a small dog or when starting out at a low height with a novice dog. The following plan can be used to construct a table with a PVC base of either permanent or adjustable height. The plywood top slides over the base to complete the table. (See Figure 5.)

Tools

- Hacksaw or heavy-duty pipe cutter (appropriate for 1 ½-inch [3.8-cm] pipe)
- Tape measure
- Marker
- Clamps and worktable
- Circular saw or table saw, or find a friendly home improvement center willing to cut lumber and plywood
- Drill with drill and driver bits
- Paintbrushes, rollers, and disposable trays

Figure 5

Materials

- 2 10-foot (3.0-m) lengths of 1 ½-inch (3.8-cm) schedule-40 PVC for construction of base plus legs for 8-inch (20.3-cm) height
- 1 10-foot (3.0-m) length of 1 ½-inch (3.8-cm) schedule-40 PVC for legs, *if* table will be any taller than 8 inches (20.3 cm)
- 1 10-foot (3.0-m) length of 1 ½-inch (3.8-cm) schedule-40 PVC, *if* all three height ranges are wanted
- 2 1 ½-inch (3.8-cm) PVC four-way crosses
- 8 1 ½-inch (3.8-cm) PVC 90° ells
- PVC cement
- 1/2 sheet of ½-inch (1.3-cm) CDX plywood, cut to 36-inch (91.4-cm) square by home improvement center, if possible
- 2 2 × 4-inch × 8-foot (5.1 × 10.2- cm × 2.4-m) framing lumber
- 8 3-inch (7.6-cm) exterior screws
- 16 or 20 2-inch (5.1-cm) exterior deck screws
- Primer paint
- Exterior paint (any color), or exterior porch paint
- Paint additive to prevent skid, or a quart of fine, clean sand

Building Instructions

Table Top

1. Measure, mark, and cut two 33-inch (83.8-cm) lengths and two 36-inch (91.4-cm) lengths from the framing lumber.
2. Measure, mark, and cut a 36-inch (91.4-cm) square from the half sheet of plywood, unless you were successful in having the plywood cut for you at a home improvement center.
3. Lay the plywood top on a flat, clean surface with the rougher side facing up. Arrange the 2 × 4s (5.1 × 10.2 cm) on edge along the sides of the 36-inch (91.4-cm) top, such that the boards are flush with the outside edge of the top. You should have two 36-inch (91.4-cm) boards spanned by the shorter 33-inch boards. The boards, once attached to the top, will form a 4-inch (10.2-cm) side with the plywood and will slide over a PVC base that is 33-inches (83.8-cm) square.
4. Drill two pilot holes in each corner and drive two 3-inch (7.6-cm) deck screws in each corner to connect the square 2 × 4-inch (5.1 × 10.2 cm) assembly.
5. Carefully turn the 2 × 4 (5.1 × 10.2 cm) assembly over and place the plywood top over the 2 × 4 square. Align the plywood with the 2 × 4 (5.1 ×10.2 cm) square to be flush on all sides. Drive 2-inch (5.1-cm) long exterior deck screws through the plywood top to connect the top to the 2 × 4 (5.1 × 10.2) square. Space the screws approximately 6 inches (15.2 cm) or 8 inches (20.3 cm) apart, using five or six per side. Take care to drive the screws through the middle of the 2 × 4 (5.1 × 10.2 cm) edge (¾-inch [1.9-cm] from the edge of the board) to avoid splitting the wood.
6. Paint all sides, top, and bottom of the assembled tabletop, using a coat of primer followed by exterior paint in a color of your choice. Mix a small batch of color paint with the nonskid additive (according to the manufacturer's directions), and apply a final top coat to the top of the table. (If using sand, sprinkle a liberal coating of fine sand to the final top coat. When dry, the excess sand will fall away, leaving a rough surface.)

Table Base

1. Measure and mark eight lengths of 19-inch (48.3-cm) PVC pipe. Cut pipe with hacksaw and worktable clamp or with heavy-duty PVC cutter.
2. Clean and de-burr the PVC cut edges using medium-grit sandpaper.
3. Assemble **without glue** two identical X shapes (top and bottom of base) by inserting

Appendix I

four 19-inch (48.3-cm) lengths of pipe in each four-way cross and four ells at each end of the 19-inch (48.3-cm) PVC lengths.

4. Ensure that each 33-inch (83.8-cm) X shape assembly fits within the table top square formed by the 2 × 4s (5.1 × 10.2 cm). Also ensure that all X shapes are exactly the same size.

5. Measure and mark four legs for the base from the PVC pipe. Each leg should be 6-inch (15.2-cm) shorter than the ultimate height of the finished table. For example, to build a table 24-inch (61.0-cm) high, each of the four legs should be 18 inches (45.7 cm) long.

Figure 6

6. Clean and de-burr the PVC cut edges, using medium-grit sandpaper.

7. Repeat steps 5 and 6 for each table height desired for adjustment.

8. Assemble the legs between the PVC X shapes to complete the base.

9. Once assured of the fit, use PVC cement to glue each PVC X together permanently. (See Figure 6.)

Building a Contact Trainer

Contact obstacles, such as the teeter, A-frame, or dogwalk, are not easy to build inexpensively or store in your garage. A simple contact trainer can be built and used to train critical skills such as the "two on/two off" contact. It can also be incorporated into sequence training. The following plan results in a mini-trainer that simulates a dogwalk on one side and an A-frame on the other. (See Figure 7.)

Tools

- Hacksaw or heavy-duty pipe cutter (appropriate for 1 ½-inch [3.8-cm] pipe)
- Tape measure
- Marker
- Clamps and worktable
- Circular saw or table saw, or friendly home improvement center willing to cut lumber and plywood

- Drill with drill and driver bits
- Paintbrushes, rollers, and disposable trays

Materials

- 2 10-foot (3.0-m) lengths of 1 ½-inch (3.8-cm) schedule-40 PVC pipe
- 4 1 ½-inch (3.8-cm) PVC tees
- 6 1 ½-inch (3.8-cm) PVC 90° ells
- PVC cement
- 1 2 × 4-foot (0.6 × 1.2-m) length of a ½-inch (1.3-cm) CDX plywood sheet (equates to one half of a half sheet of plywood, preferably cut by the home improvement center)
- 1 2 × 12-inch by 6-foot (5.1 × 30.5 cm by 1.8-m) board (also preferably cut by the home improvement center)
- 1 12-inch (30.5-cm) length of 2 × 4 (5.08 × 10.2 cm) lumber stud
- 1 12-inch (30.5-cm) length of 1 × 1-inch (2.54 × 2.54 cm) lumber or a 12-inch (30.5-cm) length of ¾-inch (1.9-cm) PVC pipe
- Primer paint
- Exterior paint (any color) or porch paint
- Paint additive to prevent skid, or a quart of fine, clean sand
- 2 Exterior grade heavy-duty hinges
- 6 Exterior deck screws

Figure 7

Building Instructions

Contact Base

1. Measure and mark the lengths shown from the PVC pipe. Cut pipe with hacksaw and vice grip or PVC cutter:
2. Clean and de-burr the PVC cut edges, using medium-grit sandpaper.
3. Use two lengths of 18-inch (45.7-cm) pipe with four lengths of 8-inch (20.3-cm) pipe, together with four 90° ells and two tees, to form a square that will lie level on the

#	PVC Length
8	8 in (20.3 cm)
4	18 in (45.7 cm)

241

Appendix I

ground and form the bottom of the base. Lay the four ells approximately 20 inches (50.8 cm) apart to form the outside corners of the square. Lay the two 18-inch (45.7-cm) lengths on opposite sides of the square. Each of the two remaining sides of the square will be formed by two 8-inch (20.3-cm) lengths of pipe, connected in the middle by a tee. The tee opening should be vertical to receive the upright portion of the base. Assemble all parts to ensure a good fit.

4. Assemble the upright portion of the base by connecting two 8-inch (20.3-cm) lengths with a tee to total approximately 18 inches (45.7 cm). Repeat the process to create another 18-inch (45.7-cm) length from the remaining two 8-inch (20.3-cm) lengths and a tee. Cap each length with an ell, and insert the pipe end of each length in the tees located on the square portion of the base. Use the two remaining 18-inch (45.7-cm) lengths to span the two uprights. Connect one length to the tees located at the middle of the upright portion, and connect the last length by ells to span the top of the base.

5. Once assured of a good fit, glue all parts with PVC cement. (See Figure 8.)

Contact Planks

1. Measure, mark, and cut the wood to size, unless you had the wood cut at the home improvement center.

2. Paint all sides, the top, and the bottom of wood with a coat of primer, followed by exterior paint in a color of your choice. (Painting the wood at this stage is easier than when all parts are attached.)

3. Lay the plywood on a flat surface. Measure and mark the center of one 2-foot (0.6-m) side of the plywood. Measure and mark the center of the 12-inch (30.5-cm) piece of 2 × 4 inches (5.1 × 10.2 cm). Align the marks to center the 2 × 4 inches (5.1 × 10.2 cm) on the plywood, and clamp the two together. Carefully turn the assembly over and ensure that the clamped 2 × 4 inches (5.1 × 10.2 cm) is flush with the plywood and well centered. Drill pilot holes through the plywood and 2 × 4 inches (5.1 × 10.2 cm), and then drive 2-inch (5.1-cm) deck screws *through* the top of the plywood *into* the 2 × 4 inches (5.1 × 10.2 cm).

4. Turn the plywood assembly over again so that the attached 2 × 4 inches (5.1 × 10.2 cm) is on top. Lay the 2 × 12-inch by 6-foot (5.1 × 30.5 cm by 1.8-m) board so that it is flush and aligned with the 2- × 4-inch (5.1 × 10.2 cm) piece. Use the hinges to

The Beginner's Guide to Dog Agility

attach the long board to the 2 × 4 inches (5.1 × 10.2 cm) attached to the plywood.

5. Turn the finished plank assembly over and apply a final coat of paint, with nonskid additive to the top planks only. (If using sand, sprinkle a liberal coating of fine sand to the final topcoat. When dry, the excess sand will fall away, leaving a rough, nonslip surface.)

6. Finish the trainer by laying the plank assembly (hinges down) over the base. The hinges should rest against the top bar of the base. The space at the apex between the plywood and long board can be filled by either a scrap of 1 × 1 (2.54 × 2.54 cm) or ¾-inch (1.9-cm) PVC pipe.

Figure 8

Purchase a Tunnel and Weaves

For two agility obstacles, you just need to bite the bullet and purchase them: an open tunnel and weave poles. The tunnel, while easy for a dog to master, is invaluable when you start setting up short sequences. Weave poles are extremely difficult for your dog to learn without daily practice. Both are difficult to build or make and are a worthy investment in your new sport.

Tunnels made expressly for agility can be purchased from many catalog and Internet sources. You can save some money by purchasing play tunnels from a kid's toy store, but these will hold up only for a small dog or young pup.

Weave poles are difficult to make without access to a welder and metal stock. Although some plans exist for making weave pole sets from PVC pipe, the PVC base does not stay in place when a high-drive dog goes through. The possibility also exists that the pipe base may cause the dog to develop inefficient footwork through the poles. One alternative is to affix simple PVC poles to a stake you place in the ground at 20-inch (50.8-cm) intervals to create weave poles. These are available from numerous sources, usually at hard-to-beat prices. If you plan to play this game, however, it makes sense to treat yourself to a welded set of 12 weave poles. If you are planning to teach weaves using the channel method, you might buy a set that can be used as channels and then pushed together to form a regular set.

Agility Games at Home

With just a few pieces of agility equipment, you can practice many skills in the backyard. The following maps will give you some ideas for exercises you can set up. They are based on your having a minimum of three jumps, one open tunnel, one set of weave poles, and a table. (If you have trouble recognizing the symbols, review Chapter 2, where they are identified.)

Each exercise has a mirror image. Make sure to practice the exercises in both directions, so that your dog is equally comfortable with turning right or left and with you handling on either side.

Here's how to read the maps (Note: Each space on the grid is 10 × 10 feet [3.0 × 3.0 m]):

■ A single symbol for handler and dog indicates the starting position for the exercise. A single handler indicates you can complete the exercise on one side, using only your right or left arm.

■ Multiple symbols for the handler show the handler switching sides (and arms) using a front or rear cross.

■ The line indicates the path the dog will travel to complete the exercise.

■ Numbers in the more complicated exercises indicate the order of the obstacles as well as the side of the obstacle your dog should perform.

■ More than one number on the same obstacle means that your dog should perform the obstacle more than once. The dog may perform the obstacle in the same direction or the opposite direction, which will be indicated by the position of the number. For example, in the first exercise, your dog will take the same jump in the same direction twice.

Once you complete these exercises, you can rearrange just these few obstacles to make hundreds of mini courses. When doing each exercise, use your verbal commands and your body language to communicate with your dog. Remember to use your voice and positive reinforcement to ensure that your dog enjoys the game. Always end your practice before your dog (and you) gets tired and frustrated.

Jumping Exercises

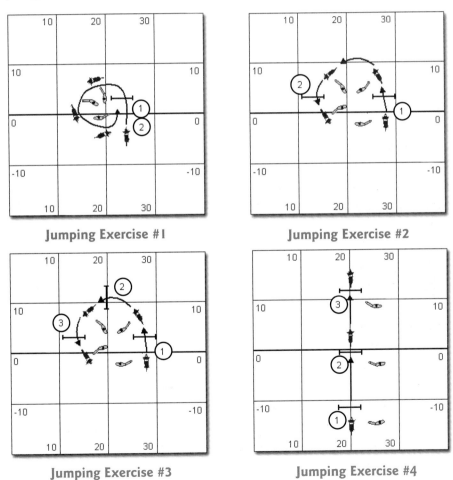

Jumping Exercise #1

Jumping Exercise #2

Jumping Exercise #3

Jumping Exercise #4

Appendix II

Tunnels and Jump Exercises

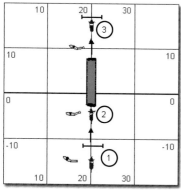

Tunnel and Jump Exercise #1

Tunnel and Jump Exercise #2

Tunnel and Jump Exercise #3

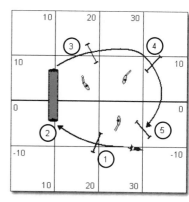

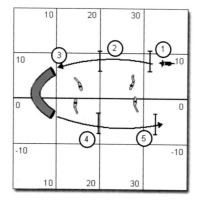

Tunnel and Jump Exercise #4

Tunnel and Jump Exercise #5

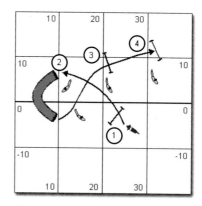

Tunnel and Jump Discriminations

The following exercises are designed to begin teaching your dog to discriminate between obstacles. In both cases, you are teaching the dog that, even if a tunnel is staring him in the face, it is not always the correct obstacle.

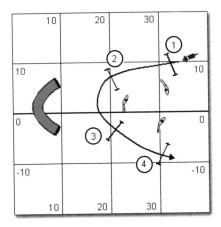

Discrimination Exercise #1

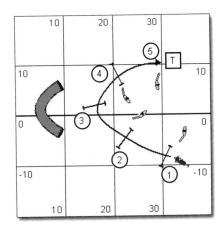

Discrimination Exercise #2

Front Cross Exercises

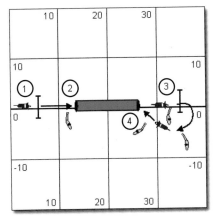

Front Cross Exercise #1

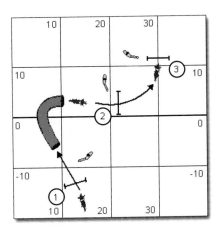

Front Cross Exercise #2

Appendix II

Rear Cross Exercise

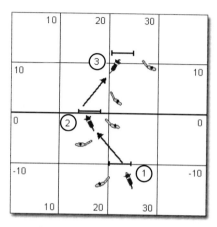

Rear Cross Exercise #1

Longer Sequences

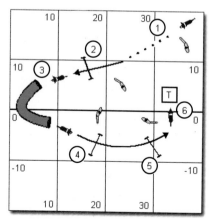

Longer Sequence #1

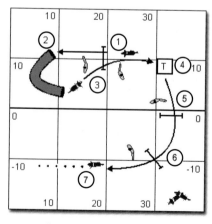

Longer Sequence #2

The Beginner's Guide to Dog Agility

Agility Association of Canada (AAC)
Secretary: Donna Kloc
E-mail: maplelass@yahoo.ca
www.aac.ca

American Kennel Club (AKC)
260 Madison Ave
New York, NY 100
Telephone: (212) 696-8200
www.akc.org

Australian Shepherd Club of America (ASCA)
Secretary: Ann DeChant
E-mail: ann@sundewfarm.com
www.asca.org

Canadian Kennel Club (CKC)
89 Skyway Avenue, Suite 100
Etobicoke, Ontario
M9W 6R4
Telephone: (416) 675-5511
E-mail: information@ckc.ca
www.ckc.ca

Canine Performance Events, Inc. (CPE)
E-mail: cpe@charter.net
www.k9cpe.com

Dogs on Course in North America (DOCNA)
E-mail: info@docna.com
www.docna.com

The Kennel Club
1 Clarges Street
London
W1J 8AB
Telephone: 0870 606 6750
Fax: 020 7518 1058
www.the-kennel-club.org.uk

Northern American Dog Agility Council (NADAC)
E-mail: info@nadac.com
www.nadac.com

United Kennel Club (UKC)
100 E Kilgore Road
Kalamazoo MI 49002-5584
Telephone: (269) 343-9020
Fax: (269) 343-7037
E-mail: dvavla@ukcdogs.com or
mmorgan@ukcdogs.com
www.ukcdogs.com

United Kingdom Agility
Langdale
Church Street
Offenham Evesham Worcestershire
WR11 8RW
Telephone: 01386 424218
E-mail: info@ukagility.com
www.UKAgility.com

United States Dog Agility Association (USDAA)
P.O. Box 850955
Richardson, TX 75085
Telephone: (972) 487-2200
Fax: (972) 272-4404
www.usdaa.com

249

Note: Boldface numbers indicate illustrations; italic *t* indicates a table.

A-frame and dogwalk, 19, 20, **20**, 61, 74, 80, 107–125
  beginner's height for, 113–114
  commands for, 109
  contact areas in, 108, **108**, 115–116, **115**, **117**
  downside contact zone in, 116
  falls from, preventing, 112
  height of, 111, 113–115
  pausing at top of, correcting, 186–187
  purchasing, 110
  running contact in, 123–125, **123**, **124**
  speed on, 110–113
  successful training in, 109, 117
  touch command in, 122
  two-on/two-off landings for, 117–123, **118**, **119**, **121**
  two-part training in, 108
  upside contact zone in, 115–116
  Walking the Plank game, 113
adult dog adoption for agility training, 39
advanced beginner sequence course, 178–181, **179**, **180**, **181**
advanced level, 11
age of dog, 34–35
Agility Association of Canada (AAC), 15, 204, 249
agility games, 244–249
  front cross exercise for, **247**

jumping exercises in, 245, **245**
rear cross exercise, **248**
sequencing exercise, **248**
tunnels and jumps exercises for, 246–247, **246**, **247**
agility schools, 71–77
  basic skills learned at, 74
  breed differences and, 74
  characteristics of effective teachers in, 72
  communication is important in, 74
  individual instruction in, 74
  multiple teachers and, 77
  novice dogs and, 73
  obedience and control requirements for, 73
  obstacles used in, 72–73
  positive training used in, 73
  practice and homework from, 75
  private vs. group instruction in, 76–77
  questions and answers during, 75
  resources and tools for, 75–76
  safety and, 72
  seminars and camps for, 77
  strategies used in, 75
agility *stay* command, 53–56, **56**
American Kennel Club (AKC), 11, 14–15, 95, 204, 249
  Indefinite Listing Privileges (ILP) from, 39
applause and praise for competitors, 230
arms used in body language commands, 160–162
attending trials, 202–203

Australian Shepherd Club of America (ASCA), 15, 249

bar knocking, 92, 189–190, 191*t*
beds and bedding, 209
beginner sequences course, 174, **174**
beginning in agility, 17
body language commands, 66–69, 159–166
  arms used in, 160–162
  backward and forward in, 67–68
  bowling your dog thru using, 160–161, **161**
  changing position using, 162–166
  close command in, 69
  drawing a path using, 161, **161**
  eyes used in, 160
  feet used in, 162
  front cross using, 163–165, **163**, **164**
  lead out using, 162–163, **162**
  leg weaves in, 68, **68**
  pushing the dog away using, 161–162, **161**
  rear cross using, 165–166, **165**, **166**
  sequencing training and, 177
  shoulders used in, 160
  spins in, 68–69
  through your legs practice in, 68, **68**
  timing for, 167
  turn command in, 69
  verbal commands vs., 157–159
  watching your dog for, 160
bones and joints, growth plates and competition, 33

bowling your dog using body
    language, 160–161, **161**
breed differences and agility training,
    74
briefings, 137, 220
broad jump, 87, 94
build your own agility equipment,
    234–243
    contact trainer, 240–243
    jumps, 235–237, **235**, **236**, **237**
    tables, 237–240, **238**, **240**

call-off, 193
camps for agility training, 77
Canadian Kennel Club (CKC), 204,
    249
Canine Performance Events (CPE), 15,
    17, 34, 204, 249
cavaletti training for coordination,
    65–66
celebrating with your dog, 223
CERF, 37
chairs for trials, 209
challenges in training. *See* training for
    agility
changing position using body
    language commands, 162–166
channel method of training weave
    poles, 147–151, **148**, **149**, **150**
checking in at trial, 217
checking your dog's readiness for
    agility trials, 213–214
chutes. *See* closed tunnels (chutes)
class organization, 11, 17, 43, 220
cleaning up after your dog, 229
clicker training, 45–47
close command, 69
closed tunnels, 22, **22**, 99, 102–103,
    102. *See also* tunnels
collar weave approach to training
    weave poles, 146–147, **147**

collar-holding tips, 69
collars, 222
come (recall) command, 50–51, **51**
comfort issues, at trials, 203–205, 211
confidence, 31
conformation and agility competition,
    33
contact obstacles, 19–20, **20**, 80
    Four-Paw Rule, 220
contact trainer, build your own,
    240–243
contact zones, 108, **108**
    A-frame and dogwalk, 115–116,
        115, **117**
    blowing or missing, 187–188, 189*t*
    running contact for, 123–125, **123**,
        124
    teeter, 129–130
    two-on/two-off landings for, 117–
        123, **118**, **119**, **121**
cooling down your dog after
    competition, 224
coordination training, 64–66
correction-free training methods,
    42–43
courses for agility competition, 11
crates, **63**, 208
criticizing others at trials, 231
crosses, cross-overs using, body
    language commands, 163–166,
    163, **164**, **165**
Crufts Dog Show and agility history, 10

deaf dogs in agility, 34
degrees in agility. *See* scoring
distance between weave poles, 151
dog beds, 209
dog interactions at trials, supervising,
    228
dogs suited for agility, 12, 13–14,
    29–39

age and, 34–35
confidence in, 31
conformation and, 33
deaf dogs as, 34
drive (high or low) and, 36
energy level requirements for, 30
eyesight and, 34
health and, 33–34
interest in working with you and,
    31
physical characteristics of, 32–35
positive attitude toward other dogs
    and, 32
prey drive requirements in, 31
psychological characteristics of,
    29–32
trust of people and, 31
weight and, 35
willingness to run requirements for,
    30–31
Dogs on Course in North America
    (DOCNA), 15, 204, 249
dogwalk. *See* A-frame and dogwalk
down command, 52–53, 139–141,
    139, **141**, 192–193
drawing a path using body language,
    161, **161**
dressing for agility trials, 210
drive, high vs. low, 36
drop command, 64
dysplasia, 37

earning titles, 225
elbow dysplasia, 37
energy level requirements, 30
entries to tunnels, challenges of,
    104–105, **105**
etiquette of agility competition,
    227–231
evaluating your performance, 224–225
exercise pens, 208, **208**

eyes used in body language commands, 160
eyesight, in dog, 34, 37

fear of judge, 191–192
feet used in body language commands, 162
food or treats in training, 44–45, 55, 229–230
Four-Paw Rule, 220
friends in agility, 209–210
front cross using body language commands, 163–165, **163**, **164**, **247**
fun matches, 200–201

gamblers courses, 23
games for agility, 23–24, 244–249
go on command, 66
growth plates, 33

halters, head type, 59
handling skills, 12, 157–169
  body language used in, 159–166
  mistakes in, 169
  rules for, 168–169
  sides, working your dog equally on left and right, 168
  timing of commands in, 167
  toys used in, 168
  verbal commands vs. body language in, 157–159
harnesses, 59
health issues, for trials, 203–205, 211
health of dog and agility, 33–34
heel command, 56–58
height, 89, 95
  A-frame and dogwalk, 111, 113–115
  dog vs. height of obstacles, 11
  jumps, 87, 95, 216–217

measuring your dog's, 202, 217
teeter, 129, 131–132
withers as measure of dog's, 95
high-drive dogs, 36
hip dysplasia, 37
history of agility, 10

ice chests, 209
Indefinite Listing Privileges (ILP), 39
interest of dog in working with you, 31
intermediate level, 11
Internet sources of information, 15

jump commands, 88
jumpers courses, 23, 85
jumps, 21, **21**, 43, 80, 84, 85–95
  adding angles to, 93
  adding jumps to, sequencing of, 93
  bar knocking in, 92, 189–190, 191t
  broad, 87, 94
  build your own, 235–237, **235**, **236**, **237**
  commands for, 88
  exercises for, 245, **245**, 246–247, **246**, **247**
  height of, 87, 89, 95, 216–217
  practicing, 89
  purchasing, 86
  recall phase in training for, 89–90
  running with your dog for, 90–91
  send on phase of, 91–92
  single, 87
  spread, 87, 93
  successful training in, 85–86
  teaching single-bar and panel type, 88–93
  tire, 87, **87**, 94–95
  wings on, 88
  young dogs and, 89

keeping it fun, 95
Kennel Club (KC), 204, 249
knocking bars off jumps, 92, 189–190, 191t

ladder game for coordination training, 64–65
lateral position of handler, 91
lead out using body language commands, 162–163, **162**, 176–177
leashes, 222, 229
left/right side, working your dog equally on, 168
leg weaves, in body language training, 68, **68**
let's go command, 58–59, **58**
locating trials, 214–215
low-drive dogs, 36

Meanwell, Peter, 10
measuring your dog, 202, 217
memorizing the course, 218

noise tolerance training, 62–63
nonqualifying (NQ) runs, 225
North American Dog Agility Council (NADAC), 13, 15–16, **15**, 17, 34, 95, 201, 204, 249
Novice Agility Jumpers (NAJ), 225
novice class, 11
  agility schools and, 73
  standard course for, 24–27, **24**

obedience training for agility, 49–59
  agility *stay* command in, 53–56, **56**
  body language used in, 159–166
  come (recall) command in, 50–51, **51**
  down command in, 52–53
  drop command in, 64

The Beginner's Guide to Dog Agility

establishing proper groundwork for, 59

go on command in, 66

heel command in, 56–58

let's go command in, 58–59, **58**

release words used in, 59

sit command in, 52–53, **52**

Sphinx down command in, 53, **54**

verbal commands vs. body language in, 157–159

obstacles, 12, 19–21, 80–83

A-frame as. *See* A-frame and dogwalk

agility school use of, 72–73

building your own. *See* building your own agility equipment

contact obstacles, 19–20, **20**, 80

dogwalk as. *See* A-frame and dogwalk

Four-Paw Rule for, 220

height of, 11

home practice with, 81

introduction to, 82–83

jumps as. *See* jumps

on-leash work with, 82

pausing or stopping training in, 81

standard novice course using, 24–27, **24**

table as. *See* tables

teeter as. *See* teeters

tunnels as. *See* tunnels

weave poles as. *See* weave poles

working with a partner on, 81

OFA, 37

off-course disqualification, 159

on-deck area, 229

on-leash work, 82

open tunnels, 21, **22**, 98, 99–102

organizations for agility competition, 14–15

other dogs, positive attitude toward, 32

packing for trial day travel, 207–211

pairs courses, 23–24

parking lot etiquette, 228

partners for obstacle work, 81

pausing on A-frame, 186–187

pedigrees, Indefinite Listing Privileges (ILP) and, 39

physical characteristics of the good agility dog, 32–35

play, 63–64

popularity of agility, 9–10, 13

positive reinforcement in training, 14, 41–47, 73

practice jumps at trials, 228–229

practicing agility at home, 75, 81, 89, 244–249

premiums, filling out, 215–216

preparing your dog for trials, 220–221

prey drive requirements, 31

private vs. group instruction, 76–77

progressive retinal atrophy (PRA), 34

psychological characteristics of good agility dogs, 29–32

puppies

estimating agility potential in, 37–39

growth plates and bone health in, 33

jump training and, 89

socialization of, 61–63

weave-pole training and, 146

push-pull approach to training weave poles, 146

pushing the dog away using body language, 161–162, **161**

qualifying (Q) runs, 225

rear cross using body language commands, 165–166, **165**, **166**, **248**

refusals, 167

registering your dog for agility, 199–200, 204*t*

Indefinite Listing Privileges (ILP) and, 39

release words, 59

reservations, 217

resources and information on agility, 249

resources and tools for agility training, 75–76

rule review before trials, 201–202

run, in competition, 43

running contact, 123–125, **123**, **124**

running off course, 193–194, 195*t*

running the course, 223

running, dog's willingness to, 30–31

safety and agility training, 72

scoring, 12

seminars for agility training, 77

send on, 91–92, 100–102, 103–104

sequencing, 171–181

advanced beginner sequence course for, 178–181, **179**, **180**, **181**

basic guidelines for, 173–174

beginner sequences in, 174, **174**

body language commands used in, 177

exercise for, **248**

Lead Out used in, 176–177

readiness for, assessing your dog, 171–172

teaching, 175–176

timing of commands for, 178

toy or food bag use in, 176

verbal commands used in, 177

setbacks in training, reasons for, 183–185

setup at trial, 217, 227–228

shoulders used in body language

commands, 160
single jump, 87
sit command, 52–53, **52**, 139–141,
   139, **141**, 192–193
skill levels, 11
socialization, 61–63
speed, on A-frame and dogwalk,
   110–113
Sphinx down command, 53, **54**
spinning behaviors, 67, 68–69
spins, in body language training,
   68–69
spread jump, 87, 93
standard novice course, 23, 24–27, **24**
start line problems, 188–189, 190t
Starts Standard Agility (SSA), 225
stay command, start line problems
   and, 188–189, 190t
stressed dogs and problem behaviors,
   194–195
supervision dog interactions, 228

table, 22, **22**, 80, **134**, 135–141
   build your own, 237–240, **238**, **240**
   down or *sit* command for, 139–141,
      139, **141**
   problem solving for, 140
   purchasing, 136
   refusing to sit or down on, 192–
      193, 194t
   running to and getting on, 137–139
   successful training in, 136
   teaching, 137
tabs (leashes), 80, 94
team work, dog and human, 31
teams for agility competition, 11
teeter, 19, 20, **20**, 80, 127–133, **126**
   beginner's height for, 129
   commands for, 128
   contact zones in, 129–130
   fear of, 133

height of, 129, 131–132
patience in training for, 133
preparing for, 128
problem solving for, 132–133
purchasing, 128
sound sensitivity and, 130
successful training in, 127
teaching, 128–129, **129**
tents and tent floors, 208–209, **209**
through-your-legs practice in body
   language, 68, **68**
tieing your dog, 230
timing of commands, 167, 178
tire jumps, 87, **87**, 94–95
titles in agility, 225
tools for agility training, 75–76
touch command, 122
toy play in training, 44, **44**, 63–64,
   176
toys, 168, 222
training for agility, 11, 41–47
   adult dog adoption for, 39
   agility schools in. *See* agility
      schools, 71
   body language used in, 66–69,
      159–166
   breed differences in, 74
   cavaletti training for coordination,
      65–66
   challenges of, 43, 183–195
   clicker type, 45–47
   commitment to, 20, 38
   common problem issues in,
      185–195
   contact zone problems and, 187–
      188, 189t
   coordination training in, 64–66
   correction-free methods in, 42–43
   current vs. new dog for, 35–36
   dogs best suited for agility. *See*
      dogs suited for agility

drop command in, 64
fear of judge and, 191–192
food or treats in, 44–45, 55
go on command in, 66
jump commands, 88
jump problems and, 189–190, 191t
Ladder game for coordination,
   64–65
noise tolerance in, 62–63
pausing at top of A-frame and,
   186–187
play and, 63–64
positive reinforcement methods in,
   14, 41–47, 73
pre-agility training and, 61–69
running off course problems,
   correcting, 193–194, 195t
setbacks in, reasons for, 183–185
socialization as, 61–63
start line problems and, 188–189,
   190t
stressed dogs and, 194–195
table problems, 192–193, 194t
toy play in, 44, **44**
verbal commands vs. body
   language in, 157–159
weave pole problems and, 185,
   186t
"Whee" attacks and, 190–191, 192t
treats in training, 44–45, 55, 176,
   229–230
trials, 199–205, 212–225
   applause and praise for competitors
      at, 230
   attending, 202–203
   briefings for, 220
   celebrating with your dog after, 223
   checking in for, 217
   checking your dog's readiness for,
      213–214
   class check-in for, 220

The Beginner's Guide to Dog Agility

cleaning up after your dog at, 229
collars and leashes, 222
cooling down your dog after, 224
criticizing others at, 231
dressing for, 210
earning titles in, 225
etiquette for, 227–231
evaluating your performance after,
224–225
final preparations for, 222
fun matches and, 200–201
health and comfort issues for,
203–205, 211
jump heights and, 216–217
locating trials for, 214–215
measurements taken for, 202, 217
memorizing the course for, 218
on-deck area at, 229
packing for, 207–211
parking lot etiquette for, 228
practice jumps at, 228–229
premiums for, filling out, 215–216
preparing your dog for, 220–221
prompt arrival at, 229
registering your dog before, 199–
200, 204t
reservations for, 217
reviewing trial schedule for, 218
rule review for, 201–202
running the course, 223
setup at, 217, 227–228
supervising dog interactions at, 228
tieing your dog and, 230
treats and toys, 222

trial workers for, 230
walking the course in, 219
work schedule sign up and, 217,
231
trial workers, 230
trust of people, 31
tug games, 63–64
tunnels, 21–22, **22**, 80, 97–105, 243
closed (chutes), 99, 102–103, **102**
commands for, 99
entries to, 104–105, **105**
exercises for, 246–247, **246**, **247**
ignoring, teaching your dog to run
past, 101
open, 98, 99–102
purchasing, 98
recall phase in, 100, 102–103
running with your dog through,
100, 103
send on phase of, 100–102,
103–104
successful training in, 98
types of, 98–99
turn command, 69
two-on/two-off landings, 117–123,
118, 119, 121

United Kennel Club (UKC), 16, 34,
204, 249
United Kingdom Agility (UKA), 204,
249
United States Dog Agility Association
(USDAA), 11, 16, 17, 34, 95, 204,
249

vaccinations, 33–34
Varley, John, 10
verbal commands vs. body language,
157–159, 177
vocabulary of agility, 12
volunteering to work at trials, 231

walking the course, 219
walking the plank game, 113, 128
weave poles, 22, **22**, 80, **142**, 143–
155, 243
age limitations for, 146
channel method of training, 147–
151, **148, 149, 150**
collar weave approach to training,
146–147, **147**
commands for, 145
distances between, 151
new developments in teaching, 151
popping out of, correcting for, 185,
186t
purchasing, different types of, 144
Push-Pull approach to training, 146
successful training in, 145
weight and agility, 35
"whee" attacks, 190–191, 192t
willingness to run requirements, 30–31
wings, on jumps, 88
withers, as measure of dog's height,
95
work schedule sign up at trials, 217,
231

About the Author

Laurie Leach is an agility competitor on the national level. She has also competed in obedience trials and raced sled dogs. Creator and writer of the award-winning website, www.laughingdogpress.com, she has also developed a subscription-based webzine for beginning agility competitors. She is a member of the Dog Writers Association of America and is a speaker at dog-related events. Laurie lives in Windsor, California.

Acknowledgments

I consider myself fortunate to have found several outstanding teachers. Many of their ideas and examples are included in this book.

A special thanks to Debbie Stoner, who laid the groundwork for my understanding of agility. Also, a major thanks to Lauri Plummer, who deepened my understanding of agility with her thoughtful approach to dog training, and who graciously allowed me to include many of the training ideas she has shared with me in this book.

My deep appreciation goes also to agility competitors and writers Kathy Wheelock, Connie Tuft, Deb Eldredge, DVM, and Sharon Freilich. Their work is woven into these chapters.

I am indebted to Celeste Thomas for her thoughtful editing and feedback of every chapter from a novice competitor's perspective.

Photo Credits

Photos on pages 8, 10, 12, 14, 16, 18, 28, 34, 37, 40, 42, 70, 80, 84, 86, 87 (bottom), 96, 99, 106, 111, 112, 126, 130, 141, 142, 145, 154, 182, 183, 184, 187, 189, 196 (top), 198, 206, 212, courtesy of Doghouse Arts

Photos on pages 119 and 205 courtesy of Phil Freilich.

Photo on page 223 courtesy of Tracy Kinney.

Photos on pages 20, 21, 22, 81, 85, 97, 107, 127, 135, and 143 courtesy of Laurie Leach.

Photos on pages 5 (second from top and bottom), 7 (top right), 30, 32, 52, 54, 60, 68, 72, 74, 76, 83, 87 (top), 91, 93, 98, 102, 104, 108, 115, 117, 118, 123, 124, 129, 132, 137, 138, 139, 147, 148, 149, 150, 156, 158, 161, 162, 164, 167, 169, 170, 172, 173, 188, 193, 196 (bottom), 201, 202, 209, 218, 221, 226, and 228 courtesy of Ellen Perlson.

Photo on page 5 (third from top) courtesy of Ann Clayton Photography.

Photo on page 210 courtesy of Laurel Putnam.

Photo on page 121 courtesy of Richard Reynolds.

Photos on pages 45, 196 (far left), and 217 courtesy of Julie Snyder.

Photo on page 5 (top) courtesy of Tien Tran.

Cover photos courtesy of Ann Clayton Photography (bottom left), Ellen Perlson (top right and center), Doghouse Arts (bottom right), and Isabelle Francais (top left and top center).

All other photos courtesy of Isabelle Francais and T.F.H. archives.